Maureen Egan is not merely a cancer survivor, but a waymaker through the dark turns of her journey with breast cancer, the luminosity of her words and her original painting guiding the way in her memoir, *The Light from Here*. She strives to be brave, but more importantly, honest. She shares the struggles cancer brings and accentuates in her marriage, and the joy and occasional hardship of being a mother, a wife, and an artist—always circling back to the gift of it all. Her bright spirit is perhaps best revealed through the number of family members, friends, strangers, and healers who hold the space for her to move back into the light. *The Light from Here* is a book for all souls who are striving to heal from cancer, and all those who have survived—women and men. She and her memoir are gifts to all of us striving to keep to the light.

—Frank O Smith, author of *Dream Singer*

Maureen Egan notices the small and important things and knows what to do with them, both as a person and as a writer. Because *The Light From Here* is so well written, it reads fast, but it deserves and rewards the kind of attention that Egan gives to the brutal surprises that life gives her. Her searingly honest account of her confrontation with breast cancer pulls the reader along, gracefully shining light on the sources of her strength. If men who care about women read one book this year, it should be *The Light From Here*.

— Ned Bachus, author of *City of Brotherly Love* and
Open Admissions: What Teaching at Community College Taught Me About Learning

This brave and beautiful book will be a blessing for anyone struggling to deal with or understand cancer and its treatment. Maureen Egan creates, with words and painting, a vivid, heartbreaking and ultimately triumphant travelogue of her journey back to wholeness.

—Dave, Morrison, author of *Cancer Poems* and *Shake Hands with your Heart*

Maureen Egan shares her intimate journey through breast cancer treatment against the evolving landscape of her emotional interior. Richly multilayered, the book interweaves the author's art and storytelling to describe family relationships, personal growth, and health challenges as she confronts anxieties about her worth, marriage, and resilience. Her symbolic paintings are powerful, and her writing, honest and poignant. Hers is an authentic story which will remind all of the healing power of love and resonate with anyone on this journey.

—Sally Loughridge, author of *Rad Art: A Journey Through Radiation Treatment*

She drew me in and took me on her journey with such beauty of language, such power and honesty and courage and love. There was so much to relate to, learn from, and be inspired by. Her words and art have touched me and changed me. I will be forever grateful—and, I'll be sharing this book. —Kate O'Neill

I felt like I was in a cocoon of love the entire time I was reading it. The love Maureen shares is contagious. —Carol Miller

This is not just a breast cancer story, it's a cancer story, and a love story, and a story of strength and humor and giving. —Barbara Spaulding

I fell in love with this book. I read it straight through, cover-to-cover, as soon as I got it. The art is beautiful. The writing is truthful, moving, wise, and funny. —Robyn Pack

the light from here

a breast cancer story

words and images by

MAUREEN EGAN

Owl's Perch Press | Rockport, Maine

The Light From Here
A Breast Cancer Story
Words and images by Maureen Egan

ISBN: 978-0-9988689-0-5

Owl's Perch Press
16 Ledgewood Dr.
Rockport, Maine 04856

© 2018 Maureen Egan
All rights reserved, including the right to reproduce this book or portions thereof in any form whatsoever. For information, contact above address or visit TheLightFromHere.com.

Cover photo by Maggie Churchill. Book design by Tim Seymour Designs, LLC

Owl's Perch Press softcover second edition, June 2018

Manufactured in the United States of America

For Dad, who gave me words,

and Mom, who gave me will

Author's Note

I wrote this book for breast cancer patients and the families, friends, and medical teams supporting them. The current statistic is that one in eight women will be diagnosed during their lifetime, women of all ages, lifestyles, and ethnicities. Although my particulars won't be a perfect match for you or your loved one, I hope you will find a thread of comfort hearing the details in one woman's story. My story is our story.

I have changed the names and identifying details of some healthcare professionals in this small state to protect their privacy and identity. I used my brother Tim's middle name, Paul, for clarity since my husband shares his first name.

For those traveling the cancer journey, whether you are the patient, the loved one, or the caring professional—whether your passage happened years ago or is ongoing, I offer my sincerest wishes for your healing.

Blessings,

Maureen

Rockport, Maine

PART ONE

Two Years Before the Diagnosis

Crisis of the Heart
July 13, 2010

I wake in a panic, in the dark, my heart wrenching from a staggering summons:

"It's over. Leave. Another life is calling."

The message is inescapable. "Leave, leave it all. Marriage. Family. Friends. Maine." It descends to my gut, sending me to the bathroom where I empty my bowels in fright.

I return to bed. Force my eyes closed. *Just breathe, Maureen, breathe.*

But I feel like I'm fighting a riptide. Rest is impossible. The water keeps pulling me from shore.

"Leave and you will find the love and purpose you seek."

Every cell seems to palpate in fear. The room is calm in contrast to the chaos within me. I hear the whir of the overhead fan and the sound of my husband Tim's breathing. I listen for my own breathing, place my hands on my chest. Wait and wait for it to settle. At last exhaustion hauls me to sleep.

Then it happens again. I wake from another cleaving of my heart. Back to the bathroom. Back to bed. I shut my eyes and try to drive the angst away with the push of each exhale. A voice in my mind intervenes. *These aren't dreams. My soul is asking me to choose. If I don't begin again, I'll never be fulfilled.*

Each time I find sleep, I'm yanked awake again—a third, fourth, fifth time. I'm taken from family, community, safety. Scenes from a new life flood in. Sunlit, brightly colored rooms, new friends, laughter, ease—all of it beautiful and effortless. It's seductive. Isn't this what I've been wanting? Could this be my fate?

When morning seeps into our room, the visions still gnaw at my heart. I'm heavy with dread as Tim begins stirring beside me, waking as on any other day in our twenty-two years of marriage, unaware that I am torn, confused, still half-believing the images that flashed before me all night. *Should I tell him of the scenes that showed me I don't belong beside him anymore? I can't. I need time to understand.* I mumble to him about having had a bad night and being tired. I say I'm relieved that I don't have to work today.

"You just rest, dee-ah," he says in a feigned Maine accent. His attempt to comfort has the opposite effect. *Can't you tell I'm a mess? Don't you know I need you to be tender?*

I get up and attempt to proceed normally, trying not to latch on to the longing that has lodged itself in my heart.

It's not who I am. It's old junk, wanting attention, craving love...promising me I'll find happiness somewhere else.

I try to eat, but after a few bites my stomach bloats. Exhausted, I retreat to my garden. It's July, warm and sunny. I sit on a spread of thyme beneath the shade of a Japanese maple. I lower my face to smell the leaves, then keep going, curling into a ball. I don't want Tim or one of the kids to find me here and ask what's going on, but I'm too weak to leave the comfort of this place. I stroke my fingers against the wooly thyme leaves. Their scent releases. I close my eyes to rest.

Sensing the Way
July 2010

That night, exhaustion brings me a deep pour of sleep, and by morning I feel renewed. Throughout the day, I try to believe that my bizarre episode has passed.

But the next night it happens again. An iceberg hits. My shell ruptures, takes in torrents. A sickening dread turns my body to lead, pressing the hope out of me so I feel like I'm sinking into darkness.

In the morning, desolate, I slide from bed early, silently, to avoid waking Tim. I tiptoe downstairs to sit in the quiet, relieved to have a meditation practice I can turn to. *You're going to be okay*, I keep telling myself, hoping to believe it. *Just let go.* It takes all my focus not to give in to the sensation of panic in my body. After twenty minutes, I feel strong enough to return to the bedroom and face Tim. I've lived with this man, mostly in harmony, for twenty-two years. I owe it to him to say something.

"I've had another bad night. I kept dreaming that I should be somewhere else. It feels so real, not like a normal dream that you can wake and walk away from. It seems more like an edict. I'm done in, and I need to be quiet. I just want you to know why."

Tim nods and stays silent. I turn away, not knowing how to be near him, afraid to confess more about the split in my personality, the part that wants to leave. I'm grateful that he is on a deadline this week in his graphic design business. This means he will be working long days and nights, out in his office at the edge of our garden, and I can keep to myself.

My nineteen-year-old daughter, Emily, approaches me as I'm leaving for work: I provide personal assistance to elderly women in the area. I can tell by her expression that she senses something isn't right with me. "What's going on?" she asks, her eyes searching me for clues.

I force a smile. "I'm not myself. Not sure why, but I feel anxious. Don't worry; I'll get help. I've got to go now."

After work, I call Gloria, a close friend I've known since our kids were young. She has given me healing Reiki sessions during difficult times, and I'm hoping she can help me again.

"Something is happening to me," I begin, and break into sobs.

"Let it out...that's right." Gloria gives me an appointment time, then urges me to go outside. "Lie on the grass and let yourself be comforted by the earth."

It's a warm afternoon. I take a light blanket to the shade of our backyard and fold myself into it. I cover all but my face and fix my gaze on the rustling leaves at the tops of the trees. Their *whsshing* is a sound of solace, and I drift into a half-sleep, dropped from time.

In my session with Gloria the next day, I lie on her massage table, clothed and blanketed. She places her hands lightly over my heart, and soon I feel their comforting warmth. She moves her hands every few minutes to rest on a new spot—lower ribcage, belly, lower abdomen, legs, top of the head, forehead, throat—all of the Reiki positions.

Gloria's voice is a steady caress as she encourages me to allow my vulnerability. "You are safe here. You can release."

Relieved of the effort of holding back, I let the tears flow.

"This is a very old pattern for you, Maureen—a hesitancy to believe in yourself. There is guilt, grief, and fear all the way to your earliest years. Love heals everything, but you must love yourself first. Then the fearful voices can be silenced."

My session with Gloria dials down the emotional intensity to a manageable level, but not for long. A pattern has commenced, and it has its own life and power. I wake with my heart racing. My legs start to vibrate, then my stomach clamps in fear. These sensations last for minutes or hours, unraveling me so that I avoid interaction, struggle to focus, have difficulty eating.

I continue to tell Tim the minimum: I'm off, feeling extra sensitive, having trouble sleeping. For once, his lack of interest in my obsessive thought patterns is welcome. I can keep to myself and avoid telling him that he is losing me to the sirens of the night. Each day I struggle to ignore the intensity of their call, and remind myself of all that I have in this life now—the foundation we've built together.

Running away doesn't solve problems. Being present allows them to be revealed.

And that's what I do. I sit on a round cushion in the quiet of each morning, drawing the air though my lungs to the deep bowl of my belly. *Take it in, let it go...take it in, release.*

I have meditated on and off for two-and-a-half decades, but *this* is advanced practice. I'm not sure how breathing and letting go of thoughts will help me through such disquieting uncertainty. I doubt I'm adept enough. I want to run.

Instead, I breathe, and it's a thread of comfort that enters my lungs and settles my heart for a moment or two, letting me know, just then, that I'm okay. *Just keep at it. Let the thoughts wash through you. Don't claim them as yours.*

The fear is less monstrous when I'm on my cushion, but when I leave the space of silence, I can turn feeble in a heartbeat. Certain sounds overwhelm me. Especially electronic sounds. Almost every noise coming from a screen—a laptop, a smart phone, the TV—keeps me on watch. Too often the sounds bring edges—cynicism, violence, dissonance—that set off my symptoms and turn my heart, gut, and limbs to buzzing cells of dread. I enter a room like a frightened animal, leaving if Tim or one of the kids is listening to music or a video. If I am in the room before they enter and then they turn on their device, I become so uncomfortable that I have to leave the space or ask them to mute the sound. I don't want to draw attention to myself this way, but anxiety and lack of sleep have weakened me, leaving me with little capacity to practice my usual measures of self-care. Avoidance is one of the few ways I can diminish the unnerving symptoms and accompanying fear.

A week into my crisis, I reach out to a therapist. Her face and body are soft and round, eyes warm and kind. If she would just sit there and smile, I might calm down. But she talks and talks, and her words are like flies buzzing around the already too warm room. *Hey, I'm paying you to help me and all your talking is making me feel worse!*

Finally, I interrupt her. "I'm really struggling. What can I do to calm myself when the panic starts?"

She pauses. "Think back to childhood. Were there smells or songs that brought you comfort? They may help you again."

I remember Rosie, one of the few material things I loved as the only girl in my family of six—the second-to-last child in a tight stack of brothers. Rosie was a tiny doll with the fragrance of her namesake, housed in a clear, plastic, perfume-style bottle with a flared red stopper that matched her hair and dress. Every time I removed Rosie from her bottle, I held her under my nostrils and breathed her in. Not wanting to weaken the fragrance, I allowed myself only a few minutes to smell her and stroke her silken hair before replacing her, recapping the bottle, and setting her back on the shelf.

Rosie is long gone, but the therapist's question prompts me to remember that a friend gave me rose-scented massage oil for my birthday. When I return home, I uncap the bottle. I inhale. My body softens.

I want to stop avoiding Tim, but I'm afraid he will say something that will trigger my angst. An idea comes. The next morning, after my shower, I tell Tim about the therapist's suggestion and about Rosie's mystique. "I need you to do something," I say, walking naked into the bedroom. "I'm going to lie on the bed and I want you to rub my heart with this oil. This isn't sexual. Pretend you're my mother and trying to soothe me."

He nods and follows me, waiting quietly while I lie down and close my eyes. In a moment, I feel the glide of Tim's fingers as he gently spreads the drops of rose oil on my chest. My heart relaxes—from the scent and the knowledge that Tim's hands have brought this relief.

Tim will perform this ritual many times in the coming weeks. Later, I'll learn that in many traditions, rose is the scent used to heal the heart.

Choosing Love
August 2010

As an artist and personal assistant, I don't have a fixed work routine. Tim, also self-employed, can never keep my schedule straight and almost every morning asks me what I'm doing that day. Today—a sultry Tuesday in early August—I tell him that I'll be with one of my ladies, then at a counseling appointment.

"I have mixed feelings about this therapist. She's nice enough, but she talks too much and I'm not sure that talking about my anxiety helps it. I think it might make it worse. Like right now, since I've brought it up, my legs are doing this weird buzzing thing."

"What do you mean—weird buzzing thing?"

I reach my hands down to my thighs, as if touching them will help me describe the sensation. "They're jittery, like they're vibrating." I make a *jjsshhzz* sound as if that will help him understand what I mean. "It's not painful, but it's very distracting." I look up at him. "It's almost as if they're turned on. You know…excited."

He steps closer. "So why don't you go with that?" His voice is serious, which is unlike him—he's so often playful and humorous—but we're several weeks into my breakdown, and he has been adjusting gradually to my own lack of humor, my anxious appeals:

"Could you turn that music off? It's too loud."

"Could you stop getting so upset about politics? It's stressing me out."

"I'm sorry, but could you listen to that show somewhere else? The sound is getting to me, and I'm trying to make dinner."

At each request, I wait for an attempt at humor that might rub me the wrong way, but to my relief it doesn't come. He simply does what I ask. And now—for a change—what I need might offer *him* something too.

"That's not a bad idea," I say, pulling off the pants I just put on. "Why not?"

I ride the urgent, restless energy. It's a relief to give it an outlet—like opening a shaken bottle of seltzer and letting the bubbles overflow. Afterward, my chest resting on his, I feel a resonance that is so calming I don't want to leave.

"I'm going to cancel my appointment today," I say, stroking his cheek. "I think I've found a new therapist."

I never reschedule. Again and again, my body turns to Tim for relief. "I need a therapy session," I whisper from my pillow at midnight or call out from the shower in the morning. Each time, he's there in a flash, always willing to take me into his arms and absorb my release. It knits our bodies together, dissolving the barriers, always ending with our chests in union for as long as time will allow.

As soon as I step away from this comfort, though, I'm vulnerable again. I'm like a switch, flipping back and forth between attraction and repulsion. On many days, an unsettling tug keeps pulling my heart away from Tim's, as if the electrons in every atom in my body are ganging up, far too convincingly, against him.

He's wearing that ratty sweater again, the one stretched out and full of holes.

Why does he call me "dee-ah" with a Maine accent? It makes me feel like an old lady.

Why won't he go dancing with me?

My silent complaints pile up. His reaction to the political climate, his preoccupation with soccer, his obsession with chocolate—they seem to tick-tock predictably like a worn, old clock.

Is this it? If we live to eighty we'll be married another thirty-one years. Oh God, I'm not sure I can bear the sameness.

One day I hear of an acquaintance who has suddenly (at least to me) left her husband for another man. I wonder what it would feel like to start over. I fantasize about finding a mate who likes more of what I like, who knows what I need. The possibility excites me, then makes me anxious, then turns into self-contempt. *Why can't I appreciate what Tim has to offer? He is so dependable and true. But why is it such work to be loving?* One day, I am so weary of the struggle I start to cry. Tim sees me and asks what's wrong.

"Maybe you'd be better off with someone who can adore you the way you deserve. I just don't know if I can be as patient with you as you are with me. Maybe I should live alone."

"You can do whatever you need to do to be happy," he says steadily. "But I know what I want. I want to be with you."

"How can you be so calm when I'm such a nutcase?"

In response, he offers a half-smile.

"The fearful voices can be silenced by love," Gloria told me once during a Reiki session.

I will try.

The next time I feel pulled away from Tim, I push forward, walk through the discomfort of my repulsion, wrap my arms around him, and press my chest to his. Moments later, I feel my heart soften as the poles magnetize back to love.

THE LIGHT FROM HERE

Realization
Fall 2010

The urge to make a new life stretches more than the bands of my relationship to Tim. At the core of my turmoil is the desire to make a more meaningful impact on the world. I recognize that this was what initiated my breakdown, was central to my angst. Friends tell me that my work as an artist and elder assistant is enough, but a restless voice inside disagrees.

For years before my breakdown, I offered various intentions in the quiet moments after meditation, asking for the confidence to overcome the blocks and fears that held me back from expressing the love I wanted to feel and share with others. As my forty-ninth birthday approached in early June, I grew urgent, telling the mysterious voice that I'd be willing to do almost anything to feel more fulfilled. I was ready for a positive new direction, not the lunacy that pulled me awake in the dark of night, revved my heart to spin like a crazed top, told me to move to New York City or New Delhi. Now, instead of embracing my future, I've become so terrified I can barely consider it.

The long, troubled nights come frequently and randomly. Bedtime becomes dread-time. The anxiety turns my stomach to stone and my thin frame grows nearly skeletal. When a friend offers a few anti-anxiety pills, I'm so at odds that I accept. On nights when I wake before midnight with my heart sinking in fear, I take a half dose and if I'm lucky, it dims the angst so I can sleep.

Mornings, I wake long before Tim, tentative about stepping into a day that may bring more pain. I proceed to my meditation cushion and begin consciously sliding the air in and out of my lungs. I'm practicing how to stay present through the discomfort I feel when the floor of my heart drops suddenly. *Don't attach. Let it pass.* I offer a breath—as sure as a mother reaching down to pick up her child—to coax it back to center. It's a relief to not have to consider anything more complicated than this.

In November, my son Cole leaves home to work at a ski resort in Colorado. Emily leaves to spend the winter on a farm in Hawaii. I claim Emily's bedroom as my studio, intending to begin my painting season, six months of making art through the long Maine winter. First, I put the garden to bed. Then I shift my gaze to the inner landscape where I hope the colors will soothe me as the plants have done through the growing season.

I'm still rather new to painting. It's been four years since I left a career grown flat to begin a self-study in art. At first I painted still lifes, but once I grew comfortable, I wanted more: a theme to explore. I began a study of the seven chakras.

Starting with the first chakra—the root chakra—I worked my way up. I created paintings that reflected the colors, themes, and symbols kindred to the corresponding energy centers in the body. This spring, I reached the fourth, the heart chakra. My heart breakdown began soon after.

Now it is time to study and paint the fifth chakra, the throat chakra, where the expression of the soul's truth through words or creative endeavors is realized. This seems fitting, but I'm nervous about starting. My legs feel the familiar buzzing, my bowels empty before I even lift a paintbrush. *What if making this painting leads to more anxiety? I'm not sure I can handle it.*

That weekend Tim and I host a woman who is teaching a storytelling workshop at a nearby school. She is willowy and pale, with long white hair pulled back in a bun. Her low voice and soft eyes captivate me. She describes how she once worked with mentally ill patients, helping them craft healing stories, which they formed together over time, a creative and therapeutic process that gave them the insights to understand and the courage to journey through their darkness.

I tell her about my own darkness. How fear has weakened me in ways I've never known.

"I'm even afraid to paint."

She nods like a lily tipping in the wind. "Here's what you can do. Begin each painting with something that creates a mood of safety. You can paint over it later, but knowing it's there will guide you."

I am soothed by her words, certain I will try.

Now, staring at the blank canvas on the easel, I recall the words of our storyteller guest. "Start the painting with something that makes you feel safe." Intuitively I place a round, glowing moon in the top right corner of the canvas, and I feel so comforted I know I won't paint over it.

Weeks pass. Outside the grass withers, the leaves turn brown. One Sunday I am sitting near our woodstove after a painting session. Tim comes to stoke the fire, then joins me on the couch. The wood crackles and hums, a sound so reassuring that I begin, at long last, the conversation that I've lacked the courage to face since my breakdown in July.

"You've been a trouper these last few months."

He stays quiet.

"I get restless—I can't help it—and every so often I need to turn the soil. But this time the ground imploded. Something inside me said I needed to leave. I was so scared. And you...you..." My voice falters and I start to cry. "These last few years, with the kids leaving home, I've felt us growing apart. We're drawn to such different things. That's okay, but I long for a deeper connection, something more meaningful."

"I don't feel those longings," Tim says with a waver in his voice. "It's enough for me to love my family. I guess I'm just a simple guy."

I take hold of his hand. "I hope you can tell I'm trying to love you better...to be more patient while we both figure out what comes next. I know you're trying, too...and I'm so grateful." I squeeze his hand and he responds in kind. I lean against his chest and let the tears come.

As the throat chakra painting nears completion, I step back from the easel. To clear my vision, I look out the window. It's a misty day, the bare trees blurred by shrouds of fog. The scene is as ethereal as the music playing in the background, Indian ragas inspired by the chakras, which repeat a slow progression of tones in hypnotic gongs and flutes. I stare at the painting, and as I do, the planes of dimension blur and I become a part of the image. The colors surround me. The waves of light enter me. The moon glows so radiantly, I forget to be afraid.

Soon after this experience, I realize the truth: I can "leave" without physically leaving. My journey will be an inner journey. I will find the connection I long for by exploring the unknown reaches of my imagination.

The Seed Within
Winter 2010 through Spring 2012

All winter and then the next I paint. I finish the chakra series in spring of 2011 and choose a new theme the following autumn: an exploration of how nature brings me solace. I use trees, animals, and colors as symbols to tell my stories. By late April of 2012, I complete my last painting of the series. I have moved slowly and steadily forward for well over a year—at work, at home, and in the studio. Still not sure where I'm headed, I am making friends with uncertainty. And like the daffodil shoots poking through the garden soil, my heart is reaching for the sun, giving me the strength to take care of something important. I have a small lump in my breast.

The lump is not new. It has been with me for more than two years. I noticed it at the far edge of my left breast a few months after I turned forty-eight, soon after my annual exam. When I found it, I experienced nothing like the sinking panic I felt when Tim noticed my first lump over a decade earlier, under the covers, right before bed. I was thirty-seven then, with two kids in elementary school, a family history of breast cancer, and a serious aversion to allopathic medicine. Then, my anxiety soared. I didn't have a doctor and had no idea how to address the foreign capsule at the edge of my right breast. It felt just like a swollen lymph node, which told me it would probably go away on its own, but the memory of my mother's and maternal grandmother's breast cancer experiences kept gnawing at me. They had both survived their postmenopausal cancers, but had found their lumps at sixty-five and seventy-five, not in their thirties.

I asked everyone I knew for the name of a doctor who practiced complementary medicine. I met the recommended doctor and was relieved when she concurred that we could just wait and watch. At the follow-up a month later, however, I was seen by her colleague. This doctor's voice was loud and breathless when she leaned over me on the examining table to say, "I treat lumps very aggressively." *Just what I was trying to avoid.* I didn't know how to stand firm against her, so I proceeded with the blood work she ordered. When she called me at work to announce that my test showed an elevated white blood cell count and that she wanted to run a battery of tests, I felt as if she were declaring war.

I knew I had to find a quieter way to approach my little lump, so I asked a retired physician friend to explain the numbers on my lab report. She showed little concern, so I decided to return to watchful waiting. In the meantime, I purchased a book by an herbalist on complementary approaches to breast cancer and studied it thoroughly. The author's reassuring tone and practical advice suited me perfectly. I incorporated a few of her suggestions, and as the weeks went by, my lump gradually shrank and disappeared. A second round of blood tests showed that my white blood cell count had returned to normal.

My second lump appeared five years later, when I was forty-two. This one came just after a nasty bout of bronchitis and once again felt like a swollen lymph node. For several months, I used the same approach as before of watchful waiting and natural remedies. But although I wasn't worried about the lump, family and friends kept urging me to have it checked. This time I chose a physician who was a breast specialist at a holistic health clinic. She palpated the lump and immediately said, "This is nothing to worry about." She did an ultrasound as well, which confirmed her manual exam. Tim and I had a high-deductible insurance policy, so my twenty-minute visit and test cost more than a week of my wages.

And then, when I was forty-eight, came lump number three. The breast specialist I had seen before had moved across the country and since this new lump felt so similar to the previous two—like a swollen lymph node—I decided to do the natural remedies and wait and watch as before.

My bean-sized lump stayed rubbery and smooth like those of the past, sometimes shrinking a bit, but then returning to its previous size. Every so often I considered having it checked, but I never followed through. I planned to have it checked at my next annual exam, but then my breakdown happened, overshadowing everything. That little lump was the least of my worries.

Month after month I dismissed it, even though I could see it when I raised my arms every morning, standing naked in front of the bathroom mirror, and even though I could find it easily when I reached under my shirt and pressed it, like a kid with a habit of biting her nails. My lump was just there, like a scar or a mole, and it didn't worry me the way other parts of my life did.

Now, after two years, the lump is changing. While the soil in our garden is thawing and softening, getting ready for the explosion of spring growth, my lump is growing dense, almost hard. It develops a tiny bump, the size of a pimple. I know from my research that these signs aren't good. Mammograms are now covered on our health care insurance, so I schedule one at our local hospital as well as a follow-up with Barbara MacDonald, a naturopath who specializes in breast cancer.

While awaiting the results of my mammogram, I begin planning for my next art show. I meet the outreach director at our local food co-op, who offers me a July slot in the cafe gallery. The co-op will host a reception, too. Cole and Emily move home for the summer. I relinquish my studio to Emily (it is her former bedroom) and point Cole toward his old room. They are twenty and twenty-three, young adults now.

A letter arrives with the mammogram results: normal. I feel somewhat relieved, but I don't know what to make of my hard lump.

I meet with Dr. Barb, the naturopath. She locates a second lump, on the same side, underneath the nipple.

"What's your intuition about these?" she asks.

"I want to believe the mammogram, but I'm concerned."

"I feel we should check into this further. I'm going to send you to a radiologist for an ultrasound." She writes instructions to send to the hospital and tells me she trusts the radiologist implicitly. "She may also do a needle biopsy if she thinks it's warranted, to draw cells to send to the lab."

Hearing this, I feel a little shaky, but I want to proceed. It's time, I know.

PART TWO

Love Breaking Through

Love's Expanse
May 31, 2012

"Do you want me to go with you?" Tim asks, referring to my appointment that morning with the radiologist.

I turn from the mirror to face him. "Are you sure? What about work?"

"Bah, work." He whooshes his hand through the air. "I'd like to come."

I'm relieved he is offering. I'm so used to taking care of health issues on my own. *Yes, I'd like that.* I lean into him, feel his warmth.

"I'm not sure what to expect or how long it will take. Dr. Barb told me they'll do an ultrasound and maybe a needle biopsy—if they need to."

We drive a half hour north, following Route 1 along the coast to Waldo County General Hospital. I have driven past this plain brick building with its square white columns many times in the thirty years I have lived in Midcoast Maine, but this is the first time I have gone in for a health procedure. A sign in the low-ceilinged, dimly lit lobby announces that this institution has recently been cited as one of the top rural facilities in the country.

I register and am taken to a room where I'm instructed to change into a johnny. Clutching it closed, I follow the young technician to a room so crammed with equipment that we have to rearrange ourselves in order to fit the four of us—me, the technician, a nurse, and a woman with hair longer and redder than my own.

"I'm Nancy Webb," she says and gives me a warm handshake. "Lovely day, isn't it? I'm thinking I'll do some planting this weekend. Do you garden?"

"Yes, I love to...especially this time of year when everything's so green." Our eyes meet and we grin. I always relax around other redheads, and I think it's mutual. It's as if we've located another member of our tribe and there is unspoken kinship.

"How are you feeling today?" she asks, and I can tell she wants the truth. Her sincerity catches me. "Oh," my voice wavers, "I'm okay," but my eyes tear up as I say so, and just as quickly, hers do too.

"Don't mind me," she says. "I'm just sensitive. If you cry, I will too." Something else we have in common. I'm not sure what role Nancy will play, but she makes me feel better. I'm glad to have her with me.

"Are you ready?" she asks.

"I guess so."

Nancy walks out of sight, but returns in a moment pulling on a white lab coat.

"I'm going to do the doctor part now, so I wear this to remind us all."

Oh, goodness, I had no idea. She's my doctor.

She settles me onto the examining table and opens my johnny. The wand of the ultrasound is cold as it circles around my right breast, then my left. Dr. Webb locates the two lumps in my left breast that Dr. Barb has indicated to her, and then discovers a third.

"I'd like to take tissue samples from each of the lumps to send to the lab," she says. She explains that she will inject a needle to draw out a few cells. She asks my permission to shoot a tiny metal marker into each lump after she finishes the injection so the location will appear later on a mammogram or MRI. The idea of this bothers me, but Dr. Webb assures me that the procedure is safe, so I acquiesce.

She turns to her nurse. "Becky, would you make sure Maureen is all prepped and cozy?" Then she touches my arm. "We'll give you an anesthetic and make you as comfortable as possible. Let us know if you aren't and we'll fix it, okay?"

Becky tucks a cotton pillow under each of my arms, then covers me with a heated cotton blanket. I close my eyes and try to deepen my breathing while Dr. Webb's steady voice instructs the technician at the computer monitor, her fingers and the instruments pressing on my breast. I stay focused on the sensation of exhalation to avoid picturing the needles going in. This works well and soon the room and its people have dissolved from my awareness. I feel no discomfort, hear no whirring machines, see no glaring light. Instead, I'm flooded with a sense of well-being that has lifted me away, taken me into another plane where only one thing exists: love. It fills my heart and surrounds me with radiance. The love is limitless, and I'm part of it. It feels better than anything I've ever encountered, dissolving my surroundings until I'm part of a field of happiness and light. I *know* that I have nothing to fear, that love is greater and more powerful than anything else. The bliss of this understanding is shattering, moving me to tears.

My tears pull me back to the room, and I hear Dr. Webb's voice trying to soothe me.

"I'm so sorry this hurts, dear. It won't be long now."

"There's no pain." I open my eyes. They're all looking at me. I smile. "I'm crying because I feel love."

"Wow," Becky says. "I want some of that."

My awareness of the room returns, with its tangle of bodies and equipment, but the glow stays with me, running in gentle currents through my limbs. I close my eyes to keep it near.

Dr. Webb stays on task, but after a while I can tell she's getting frustrated with the tool that shoots the metal markers. I open my eyes to see what this instrument looks like—a toy gun that performs just as unreliably, shooting blanks more than half the time, and making it nearly impossible for the good doctor to conceal her irritation.

"This isn't the tool I usually use," she says, holding it up to her nurse. "This thing is no good at all. Becky, where is the good one?"

"It's being repaired, Dr. Webb. This is all we have."

Dr. Webb lets out a groan. "I'm very sorry that this is taking so long. Bear with me, dear. It should only be a few more minutes."

"Take as long as you need. I'm really okay."

Becky smiles warmly, and Dr. Webb joins her for a moment before continuing on to completion.

"All done...finally!" Dr. Webb sighs. "Great job, my dear. Next stop is mammography. I know you've already had a mammo, but we'd like to take new films now that we know more. Becky, would you escort Maureen please?"

Becky takes me to a small, private waiting room and then excuses herself. I'm glad to have this space to myself, and I stand by the window, surveying the budding spring below. *What just happened to me?* The sensation was pure joy. I felt treasured and loved in a way I had never experienced before. More than that, I knew without question that I was safe. As I think more on the experience, I recall my most recent painting, *Guardian of the Lotus Girl*. I painted it to remind myself of protection. And now, my experience in the treatment room has taken me into the scene I created on the canvas, giving me what I've longed for.

It's amazing. After two years of struggling through intense anxiety, a lump in my breast has brought me the lightness of total trust. I stroke my heart, aware that this trust still surrounds me. *How can this be?*

I'm still shaking my head as the technologist calls me in for the mammogram. She has been given the location of my three lumps and is trying every angle to record them, but my breasts are small and dense, so it's hard to capture an image. Despite her cheerful efforts, the films show the same results as my original mammogram weeks earlier. No lumps detected.

She gives up at last, instructs me to change, then notifies Becky to escort me back to Tim, who has spent nearly two-and-a-half hours reading magazines in the waiting room. He looks at me and asks how I'm doing.

"It went fine. Nothing hurt. Isn't Dr. Webb wonderful?"

"Yes, she came and filled me in while you were getting changed. She's a keeper all right."

I nod, feeling grateful and relieved that he is here to take me home. On the way, I try to describe what happened during the exam, the expanse of love that flooded my body.

"Wow," he says. "I bet you weren't expecting that."

"Not at all. I hope I never forget what it felt like to have no fear."

THE LIGHT FROM HERE

Diagnosis

June 5, 2012

Five days after the needle biopsies, it's time to learn the results. Tim takes me back to the redbrick hospital and the red-haired radiologist. Her office is dark, but in a cozy way, with personal touches—family photos, art, a handmade pillow. Tim and I sit.

Dr. Webb looks at us with her soulful eyes. "It's not the news we wanted," she begins. "There is breast cancer in two of the tumors. But the tumors are small, and it's a noninvasive, slow-growing type of cancer." She looks at both of us, saying nothing more. My eyes well up with tears, and she offers her own watery eyes in response.

I'm shaken but not shocked by her news. Because of the changes in the lump, I have been half expecting it.

Dr. Webb explains the particulars of my situation. She brings out a diagram of various breast malignancies and points to the one that most resembles mine. Her tone has changed from empathy to electricity, and I realize why she does this work. Since I have already bonded with my red-haired kin, I become as fascinated as she is with my multiplying cells—how some are clumping and others are stringing together in long lines that the mammogram had great difficulty detecting. When she tells me that I have both types of cancer cells and that one type is relatively rare, I feel special, as I did in childhood when my family went to church and took up an entire pew, me the only girl and the only redhead.

As she leans toward Tim and me, making sure we're okay, Dr. Webb is family—the tribal version anyway. Her authenticity, her caring, her intelligence surround us. We are in her cave, in the center, and she is tending the fire, making sure we stay near. She is our protector, our mentor, our sister, our friend. We don't want to leave her. She doesn't make us go.

"Take your time," she says. "Most of my patients tell me later that they wish they hadn't rushed to make decisions or to take it all in."

On the drive home from Dr. Webb's, my whole body is vibrating, as if the particles of every atom inside me are re-patterning—finally freed from the fear and constriction that have plagued me for the last two years. I feel like Joan of Arc at the feet of the angel messengers, weeping at their beauty.

"This is what is supposed to happen," I say. "This is how I'll help people."

"You're right," Tim says, nodding. "You are going to be an inspiration." His eyes moisten and he turns to meet my gaze.

I'm surprised that these words are coming out of our mouths. Even more, I'm surprised to feel a strange sense of well-being, an aliveness in which all things are interconnected and I'm sure I can meet whatever obstacles arise. Surges of tenderness and self-compassion are coursing through me. Tears are dripping, sourced from the mysterious part of me that has decided—almost without my permission—to trust in the uncertainty before me.

Telling People
June 6 to June 12, 2012

Dr. Webb told me to take my time. "First, do nothing," she said. But there is one problem—I have to tell a few key people, and I don't want to because I don't want to deal with their reactions. But I should tell the people I see all the time so I won't have to hide it from them, right?

Tim has told the kids and his family. Now it's my turn.

First, I tell Elinor, who's like family even though she's my employer. Five years ago, I helped her husband, who had Parkinson's disease, during the last year of his life, and after he died I stayed on as her personal assistant. Elinor had breast cancer, too, seventeen years ago, when she was the same age as I am now. She knows about my tests and is concerned. When I share the results, I notice how her face reacts, her lips tightening and her eyes darting away. She tells me that I'm going to be fine. She got through it and it's been seventeen years and she's fine, so I'll be fine, too. She goes on for a while, repeating the word "fine" in nearly every sentence, almost like it's an order. All the while I am feeling less and less fine. A tear escapes, and she notices.

"You know I'll be here for you," she says, her eyes moistening with mine. "You just let me know what I can do."

Next, I tell a work colleague. I call her at night and can tell by her slightly slurred speech that she has had a few glasses of something.

"When I had my lumpectomy," she begins, "I had to wait forever for the results and I was a wreck, a complete mess." She tells me the whole story of her lumpectomy and its accompanying anxiety, apparently believing she's helping. To me, she feels like a puppeteer, pulling on the strings of my angst.

My mother-in-law tells me that breast cancer is not what it used to be. She lists all the women she knows who have survived, including her cleaning woman.

"Yes, the chemo was really hard and Marion lost all her hair and felt sick for months, but she survived, and you will, too."

Eventually, I realize that most people are so startled and distressed by my news that all they can think of to do is tell stories of other people they know who have survived cancer or are going through treatment. They think they're helping, but I'm not ready to hear the details of someone else's experience. I need a soft, reassuring voice, or silence, someone simply holding my hand and looking into my eyes without words. It annoys me that most people don't know how to respond, but then I realize that I need to let them know what I want.

I start sending e-mails instead of calling—even with my family and closest friends. I ask them not to tell anyone else for now because I'm still taking it in—plus I don't want to be explaining my situation in the grocery store. I'm still feeling full of love and I want to keep that feeling close. Talking about my diagnosis takes me into my head, where the fear and worry reside.

This is my first e-mail, which I sent to three of my closest friends before a dinner date together. Later I adapted it and sent it to others—including some in my family—who I thought needed to know.

Dear Ones,

Our upcoming get-together is coming at a crucial time. I had some tests last week for my two breast lumps and found out Tuesday that I have breast cancer in both. At this point, all I know is that it is a nonaggressive, slow growing type and we have caught it early. More tests and appointments are on the horizon, and decisions will have to be made. I have an MRI and blood work scheduled for Monday to get more info.

I have needed the last two days to begin to assimilate this, and I'm starting to share the news with a limited group. Please help me by keeping it between us for now, and of course, by holding me in your love.

I am grateful for my meditation practice, which is keeping me from serious unraveling. I am riding gentle waves of emotion, saturated with the love that surrounds me :-)

Of the many feelings I have experienced in the last week, one of them is feeling so blessed to have you in my life. Thank you for being who you are.

Much love,

Maureen

My intuition is right. Learning of my diagnosis via e-mail allows people their reactions without me nearby. They write back, telling me that they are holding me in their hearts, and please, they urge, let them know if there's anything they can do to help.

One friend writes that in Jin Shin Jyutsu, an ancient Japanese healing art that harmonizes the body's energy, the practitioner replaces the word cancer with "my project." *So I don't have cancer; I have a project.* I'm lightened by this news because I love projects and am curious to know how *my* project will evolve.

THE LIGHT FROM HERE

Sweetness and Sorrow
June 15, 2012

I have spotted my first hummingbird of the season! She visits my garden each morning, hovering, then darting from the salvia to the Japanese maple and back for another sip. June is when my garden peaks. Clematis, delphinium, and sages, all in shades of deep purple, bloom, and then—my favorite—the white and pale-pink peonies.

June is also our family's birthday season: me, then Cole, then Tim, all in less than two weeks. My fifty-first birthday comes a few days after my diagnosis and I celebrate quietly, still tiptoeing into my new world, getting tests that confirm that the cancer is confined to my left breast, and that I am in good health other than this diagnosis. As I learned to do with my anxiety during the last two years, I move gently during these days, tending the garden and my heart with care. I avoid doing breast cancer research on the internet or reading the packet of materials sent home by the hospital social worker. Both, I know, would fire up my fear.

By Cole's twenty-fourth birthday, six days after mine, our family is eager to come together for a meal, which hasn't happened since my diagnosis. I've asked Cole to take the night off from his job as a server. Twenty-year-old Emily, the social planner of the family, comes flying through the front door at 4 p.m.

"Let's canoe out to Curtis Island and have a picnic supper for Cole's birthday!" Right away, we know it's a go.

I remember how the Camden Hills and nestled harbors swallowed my heart exactly thirty years earlier when I arrived as a twenty-one-year-old, newly back in the states after a semester abroad, unwilling to pass the summer in my hometown in Massachusetts. A friend and I journeyed up the Maine coast during that June of 1982 with three stops planned. The last was Camden, where my brother had rebuilt a church steeple a few years earlier and raved about the people and the views. He was right. When we arrived on that spring afternoon, the harbor painted in sunlight, our choice to stay was immediate and clear.

I have lived in or near Camden almost every year since, but have only stepped onto the island at the mouth of its harbor a handful of times. It's a short boat ride from shore, but it takes enough effort to get there (loading boats on a trailer, hauling them to the public landing, then carrying them down a precariously steep hill) to make it a rare excursion for the locals who don't have a skiff—or a friend with one—in the harbor.

We're a flawless team as we secure our kayaks and canoe in the truck, pick up dinner, and arrive at the public beach just as the light starts to soften. We paddle our kayaks and canoe to the pebbly tip of the little island, tie them to a tree, then hop up the rocks to find the path that skirts the northwest perimeter.

The trail leads along a mixed stand of evergreens and spring leafing poplars to the still-active lighthouse at the eastern end of the island, facing the reach of Penobscot Bay. We scramble across granite boulders, then head back along the wide swath of lawn down the middle of the island.

"Look! A swing!" Emily races ahead. She hoists herself onto it and yells, "Push me, Dad!"

The swing has an over-sized plank seat, hanging from thick ropes tied to a tall pine. With half a dozen of Tim's running pushes it carves an impressive arc, allowing the sensation of flight. We each have a turn and when it's mine, I lean back all the way, letting Tim take me up so high that I holler with the thrill.

We spread the blanket and choose our spots. It is one of the only times since my diagnosis that we have all been together, and suddenly I feel the unease of my future—our future—quiver in my throat. Our conversation stays light and present-centered, our words tethered to the roots that bind us as a family. I make eye contact and smile at Cole, Tim, and Emily, connecting but not holding their gazes, because I am teetering, aware that as I let myself open to their tenderness and to the questions and fears that I have not fully taken in, a flood of emotion starts to rise. I want to be present for Cole on his birthday, though, to celebrate him, so I say little and try to smile.

On the paddle back to shore, I fixate on the water. Glistening crystals of light shimmer and flash, drawing me to their motion.

On our drive home, my heart sinks as rapidly as the sun, and it takes all of my focus not to cry. When we arrive, I let the others unpack our gear from the truck and then I rush to my husband's office on the edge of our property—to let go. I've no sooner crossed the threshold when sobs pour forth, collapsing me to the floor where I'm unable to stop, relieved to no longer be trying.

Now that the channels are open, all the emotions want a voice. *It's not fair. I've suffered enough. I've been through enough. I've only just left my anxious period. This is cruel. It's not right!*

I let the feelings engulf me, craving attention, imagining how family and friends will come to my aid. But then a darker, self-righteous wave rises. *People like me do NOT get cancer. I take care of myself—exercise, eat right, meditate. I'm the fucking poster child for the anti-cancer lifestyle and this is my reward? AAAAGGGGHHH!*

I sob and wail, churning in the emotional sea. It grows dark, but I don't stop. Now fear takes over. *Will it hurt? Will I lose my hair? Who will love me through this? Would dying relieve me of all this suffering? Would that be such a bad thing? No. I can't die. I can't leave Cole and Emily without a mother.*

The darkness closes in. I have gone far enough. I sit up and stare outside at the silhouetted trees. I am too spent to cry anymore. I return to the house, where Tim is already asleep. I'm relieved that I don't have to recount my descent.

THE LIGHT FROM HERE

Advice and Decisions
June 9 to June 15, 2012

I feel as if I've been planted on a four-lane highway that stretches beyond my sight—with no map. I can't keep my usual turtle pace, waiting months for the right direction to reveal itself. I've already done that and look where it got me. I need a guide, and my choice is Dr. Barb, the naturopathic doctor who sent me for the needle biopsies.

She gives me a crash course on meeting with the surgeons and how to prepare my body and mind for surgery if I decide to follow the likely course of treatment. Her knowledge of breast cancer and its treatments is encyclopedic. She writes notes for me—helpful explanations and suggestions—and even though she looks up caringly while juggling the writing and the speaking, she loses me with all the words. I push myself to keep pace with her, but my mind already feels overloaded with information.

"Have you made an appointment to see a surgeon yet?"

"Yes, with a local surgeon who's been recommended."

"I urge you to see a breast specialist, too. There are two excellent choices I can give you, both within a couple of hours drive."

I want to keep things simple, to meet just one surgeon—the local guy—to be happy with him and be done with it. I tell her this, how I want to avoid a lot of appointments, excessive driving, and decision making.

"I understand, but I think you will see a big difference when you meet a breast specialist." She explains her reasons—all good—but my brain is fogging and I'm tuning out. After our appointment, my stomach stays clenched for hours. I appreciate her advice, but I wish it didn't weigh so much. Maybe I don't want to be as prepared as she is. I've only just left my long period of anxiety and am not interested in returning to it. I'd rather lean into the unexpected bubble of trust I'm still in, where I believe that everything is happening just as it should.

For days the question plagues me. Do I stay on the quiet, two-lane road that travels comfortably through the towns I know—picking the trusted surgeon from our small, local hospital—or do I venture farther and see a specialist?

A dream intervenes that helps me decide. In it, the local surgeon walks into the examining room wearing no pants. He insists he must remove my right breast, not my left, and his slurred speech indicates he is high on something. I'm relieved when I'm startled awake, but the dream is eerily real. It highlights reservations I've been keeping at bay. I cancel my appointment with the pantless doctor, scheduling a consultation with a different local surgeon as my source of a second opinion. I also decide to accept the wisdom of meeting one of the breast specialists recommended by Dr. Barb.

I call the specialist's office that Friday, and the receptionist treats me as if I'm the only patient they have.

"We can see you Monday or Tuesday."

"Wow, that's fast." I choose a Tuesday slot.

"We try to minimize the waiting for our patients," she says. "It's part of our commitment to you."

This means that my two surgeon appointments will occur on consecutive days the following week.

Meeting the Surgeons
June 19 to June 21, 2012

The peonies in my garden are peaking on the morning of my appointment with Dr. Molin, the breast specialist recommended by Dr. Barb. On a whim, I pick an extravagant bunch of creamy-pink Sarah Bernhardts just before we leave. At regular intervals during the long drive to Portland, I brush my nose across their fragrant petals.

Because of my desire for simplicity, I still resist the idea of going this far from home. I silently judge the corporate vibe of the physician's building, and when I enter the office, I avoid all the cancer publications in the waiting area. Soon after, a nurse welcomes me to the examining room, motioning Tim to come as well. Her voice and demeanor are genuine and gentle as she hands me a johnny to prepare for my exam.

Dr. Molin knocks and enters. She is about my age, dark-haired, short, solid, and colorfully dressed, with a bright, beaded necklace that catches the light as she moves. Her brown eyes are focused and engaging as she questions me about my health history. When I finish, she grabs a pen and begins diagramming my case on the white paper covering the examining table. She speaks with the precision of her trade and uses all the terms I've been trying to avoid—in-*va*-sive carci-*no*-ma, chemo-*ther*-apy, radi-*a*-tion, fu-ture *can*cer, lymph node in-*volve*-ment—but her directness and soft Brooklyn accent sow trust rather than alarm.

After she examines me, I dress and we convene in a small room, brightened by sunlight and warm colors, outfitted with comfortable armchairs and large, framed artwork that harmonizes with the furnishings. Without medical equipment and a johnny as barriers, I feel Dr. Molin's equal.

"Since you have two tumors on the same side and a small breast, it's prudent to do a single mastectomy," Dr. Molin says once we've settled in, explaining why she has recommended this course and isn't overly concerned with recurrence.

"The main reason to remove the other breast would be to do reconstruction. I don't mean to be flip, but some people see this as a chance to get an augment." Her lips curl amiably, and I quickly respond with, "Don't think I haven't thought of that!" We laugh together, and then she describes the reconstruction process, how she would have to remove all of the tissue of the healthy breast during my surgery, causing me to lose most of the sensation on my right side in addition to my left. It would take multiple visits with a plastic surgeon over a period of many months to gradually stretch the skin and muscle for the temporary implants, which would be replaced with more permanent ones once the correct size was reached.

I have been toying with the novelty of getting a free boob job, but the more she details the process, the less enticing it feels. Her description makes me realize what I would lose rather than gain. It is clear to me that I'd rather keep the pleasure sensors alive on my tiny-but-good breast than have two curvaceous but unfeeling ones. Once I express this, Dr. Molin weighs in. "Your chances of recurrence are low, and if you keep your right breast, you'll be able to enjoy it. The only reason to do reconstruction is to preserve your sense of being intact, your identity, or womanliness, if you will, but it involves more surgery, more complications. It has to be worth it to you."

"Probably not," I say, and then sigh. "I'm a pretty natural person and hearing all this makes me realize what is best for me. I've been flat chested my whole life; I'm used to it."

I explain to Dr. Molin that I have an art show opening scheduled for July 11, nearly four weeks away. "It's really important for me to schedule my surgery for after my opening, and maybe this sounds funny to you, but I think it would be kind of cool to have the surgery on Friday the thirteenth. What better day to go under the knife, right?"

Her lips curl again and her eyes join the smile. "Friday the thirteenth is a big day for me: it's the day I gave birth to my son and is one of the happiest days of my life. I am always pumped on that day."

We all laugh. I'm so relieved that she is not concerned about waiting a month that I'm almost excited about the upcoming event, as if I've temporarily forgotten my diagnosis.

"We will schedule you for the first surgery of the morning and if all goes well, you could go home that afternoon." Tim and I exchange grins. I wasn't aware that a same-day mastectomy was possible—that I might not have to spend the night in the hospital. I'm in awe.

We stay for nearly two hours. Emily joins us partway through, and after Dr. Molin has covered all of the medical issues, she asks Emily about her life and her plans. Our conversation takes us past closing time, and we hug warm good-byes as we leave. On our way out, I notice the peony bouquet. I left it in the waiting room earlier because I felt too shy to present it to Dr. Molin upon our arrival. Now I'm ready. I hustle down the hall to her office and give her the flowers just as she prepares to lock up and go home.

I feel like skipping in the parking lot on our way to the car. I smile at Tim, knowing we have just met my surgeon. We consider canceling tomorrow's appointment with the other surgeon, but decide we should go and hear him out.

The first thing I notice about Dr. Lauer's waiting room is the lighting; the space is windowless and dim. His receptionist is wearing black, and I can't help comparing her to Dr. Molin's office assistant, whose colorful shirt mirrored her cheerful demeanor. The examining room is stark—stainless steel tables, white walls, and visceral diagrams of human anatomy surround us. As we wait and wait for Dr. Lauer, I grow uneasy and irritable. When his nurse arrives, she stands stiffly, asking questions in a monotone, her face showing little emotion.

She leaves and we wait even longer, me in my johnny, my discomfort edging toward indignation. When Dr. Lauer finally arrives, he launches in immediately. He rarely makes eye contact from behind his glasses as he lays out his plan to remove the two tumors and try to salvage my left breast. I cringe, imagining my little cutie as a deformed blob with no nipple. Then I tell him that I would like to delay surgery until after my show opening, and his response is unnerving.

"I feel we must do the surgery right away," he says. "I'd like to schedule you for next week, if possible."

"Next week?" *I'm not ready.* My stomach drops.

He is worried that the cancer might have easy access to my chest wall, and I read his grave expression as "lung cancer is just around the corner, my dear." I get defensive and remind him that my mother and grandmother both survived their postmenopausal breast cancers. His eyes finally meet mine with a watery sadness and he explains that since I'm premenopausal, my situation is more serious.

"I'm not premenopausal!" I nearly yell. "I went through menopause eight years ago when I was forty-three!" I am shocked by this. *Didn't he read my chart? How dare he pour all his doom and gloom on me, making me feel so unnecessarily afraid! Is this really the guy—so highly recommended—that people have described as warm, personable, and funny?*

He looks uncomfortable and nervous as he mumbles, "You're fifty-one? You don't look that old. I thought you were forty-three." I leave his office churning with a mixture of disbelief, anger, and self-righteousness. I am also relieved, assuming that Dr. Lauer's misreading of my age explains his dire tone.

I think of the confidence I had when I left Dr. Molin's office the day before. She predicted that there would probably be no chemo or radiation, just a surgery so straightforward that I wouldn't even have to spend the night in the hospital. But then my mind gets jittery and starts running through scenarios of fear. *What if Dr. Lauer is right? Am I just believing Dr. Molin because I prefer what she had to say?*

That night I don't sleep well. In my quiet time the next morning, steady breathing settles my nerves. *Dr. Molin and her staff have already shown me that they're here to support me through any outcome. Let go of what Dr. Lauer said. He was wrong. Just let it go.*

When I call Dr. Molin to reserve my surgery date, her voice is warm as she makes the arrangements and thanks me for the peonies. "They've cast a spell on the entire office."

Dr. Lauer calls later to rescind his concerns. He has consulted with an oncologist and realizes that he was mistaken in his assessment. I am impressed that he has taken the time to contact me, and I take his words as an apology. *No hard feelings, doc, but still, you are not the surgeon for me.*

Preparations

June 22 to July 11, 2012

We are in the peonies' last days. I linger near Sarah Bernhardt's silky petals before the rain comes and adds just enough weight, drop by drop, to lower each blossom to the ground. To avoid that sight, and the mess, I cut them to bring inside and enjoy there.

In the last two-and-a-half weeks, I've had five doctor visits, two blood draws, and my first MRI, far more medical intervention than I'm used to. But now the tests are done and my choice is made—a mastectomy with Dr. Molin just over three weeks away.

I will use this time to prepare for my art show as planned. I've worked toward this all year and Dr. Molin agrees that I don't need to rush into surgery. Relieved, I return my focus to my work.

On a sunny afternoon, I run into an old acquaintance in the village of Camden and stop to chat. I rarely see Sue and am surprised to learn that she's a big fan of my art. Her soft blue eyes brighten when she speaks of my show last year.

"Your colors are beautiful. How do you do it?"

"My paintings have a life of their own." I laugh. "They tell me what I should do next, but I'm slow, so it takes a long time and many layers of paint until I figure out what that is."

Sue is nodding, so I continue, telling her about my winter in the studio working on the theme of how nature brings me solace. "I've painted memories of real places and dreams of imagined ones, sometimes blurring the two. All the paintings have trees or animals that I have chosen for their symbolism."

We go on for a few minutes, talking so effortlessly that when Sue says, "I'd like to have one of your paintings. Can I come to your studio?" her request seems perfectly natural, as if every day I run into someone who believes in my work enough to want to purchase it.

On a bright Sunday morning I hang my paintings in a white-walled room in our house, creating a gallery for Sue. When she arrives I show her each canvas, telling its story. I'm so comfortable with her that I don't hold back the emotions that arise. My eyes well and so do hers. She chooses her painting and hands me a crinkled wad of bills as her first installment. She will go on to become one of my collectors. More importantly, this meeting has shown me that sharing my stories can be as cathartic for others as it is for me.

My session with Sue inspires me to write brief descriptions of my paintings. Tim formats a booklet for visitors to the gallery/café where my images will hang. *If I feel brave enough that night, I will talk about the paintings as I did for Sue.*

Along with my work helping elderly clients, writing the descriptions and planning the details of my show each day keep me calm, present-focused, and in the hum of creativity. The chickadee's song, the towering delphiniums, and the blue-sheeted sky overhead fill me daily, pulling me into the textures of summer. I catch a swim as often as I can, knowing I won't be in the water after my surgery, perhaps for the rest of the summer.

By the morning of the reception, I've heard from only a few friends who plan to attend. I talk myself up all day. *Everything will be all right, no matter who comes.* I picture the light-filled room with my paintings all around. When I put up my show yesterday, I was proud and pleased, a rare moment of exuberant self-approval.

I'm hoping to give a talk about my painting process during the reception, to reveal the stories that inspire my work, so that someone might be touched. I want people to know that their sensitivity can also be their strength.

On the night of the reception, my excitement is a bubbling spring. The gallery is pint-sized and can only comfortably hold about twenty bodies, which is about how many are present throughout the evening. The group includes an unexpected guest, my younger brother Paul, who has traveled all the way from southern Massachusetts to surprise me, a colorful congratulatory bouquet in hand.

When I sense that there are enough guests, I clear my throat, welcome people, and begin my impromptu talk. I move from painting to painting as I speak, and after some momentary nerves, drop effortlessly into my storytelling. The pieces are like beloved friends and their stories flow. At several points, I look out to the faces in the room and see from their expressions that I have brought them into my world—the owls, the starry skies, the curling branches, the glowing moons. At long last, I know I've found my way. Making art has helped me journey through my fear.

THE LIGHT FROM HERE

Saying Goodbye to My Breast
July 11 and 12, 2012

My breasts are soft and nearly translucent, with pale pink nipples and very little mass. I've always had mixed feelings about their size, sometimes feeling like a skinny kid, even at the age of fifty-one, still awkward in cocktail dresses with décolletage or any bathing suit designed to elicit lust.

After my diagnosis last month, when I was imagining what it would feel like to have larger breasts, free of charge, I pictured the almost-B-cup I had in the months of carrying and nursing my babies. I retrieved a black and white photograph that Tim took of my once voluptuous, pregnant breasts and propped my pin-up on our bathroom dresser so I could see them every morning going in and out of the shower. *Yes, those were mine once...a lifetime ago. Wouldn't it be nice to have them back?*

The photograph seduced me until Dr. Molin brought me back to earth by explaining that it would be much simpler to preserve the right breast—and its ability to give me pleasure. I agreed with her, accepting that I was not willing to undergo the extended period of reconstruction or to loose my mini fireball just for a set of fantasy breasts.

Now it's time to let go of my little champ, whose worth has been proven in the important ways—powerfully erogenous, and milk producing for Cole and Emily. But before I let her go, I want to throw her a party.

Years ago a friend whose cancer had recurred asked me to photograph her solo breast the day before it, too, would be taken from her. I arrived at her house as a gentle snow began to fall, climbed the narrow stairs to her bedroom, and captured her one perfectly shaped breast, bathed in gray light by the window. We laughed awkwardly at the task, but inside, I wept.

And now it's my turn. I drive to my friend Maggie's property on a steamy July afternoon, and she takes some pictures of my naked torso by a stone ledge with lush greenery. I feel silly posing—it's just not me—so after a few minutes I suggest we go skinny dipping in her pond instead.

The cool, dark water slides over my skin as I move in steady strokes to the middle of the pond. I roll onto my back and survey my frontal landscape, skin so pale it glows atop the indigo water, my nipples like pink pebbles resting on shallow mounds of sand. I tread water, luxuriating in the freedom of my nakedness, the sensuality of the chilly water against my lower body in contrast to the sun-warmed surface of the pond.

That evening, I'm still stimulated from my swim and I do what I've been waiting to do all week. I roll onto Tim and soon we are both as naked as I was in the afternoon. This is the last time my left breast will feel his tongue, his cheek, his fingertips. I allow the sorrow, the longing, the pleasure, the gratitude to rise and pass, opening my heart to an intimacy I have rarely accessed before. I hold tight, savoring, clenching, then falling into his heart and releasing my love.

The next morning is the last before surgery. I have scheduled a Reiki session with my friend Gloria to prepare for what's coming.

The padded massage table in Gloria's treatment room is draped in deep purple and blue, colors that resonate with tones of the artwork on the walls, including one of my paintings. Soon I am on that table, tucked under the covers. Gloria rests her hands on my heart and invites me to breathe deeply, leading me into a deepening state of relaxation.

In addition to being a Reiki master, Gloria is a shaman in the Celtic tradition. At times during treatment, she offers words that intuitively arise, stemming from her deep respect for feminine energy of the earth as well as an all-loving God that doesn't trigger my recovering Catholic buttons. Her voice is soft and reassuring, melding with the ethereal background music.

"Your breast is predeceasing your body. Great Mother knows this and will keep it in her care. Give her your sorrow, your anger, and your pain; her heart is wide enough to bear it all."

Through the darkness behind my closed eyes, a being appears. She is unlike anything I've ever encountered, an otherworldly presence, like a goddess or angel, but of the earth. She stands tall, with butterfly wings of kaleidoscopic colors and intricate patterns, edges blurred, details softened. Her wings stretch above and beyond my body, arching over me, offering beauty and protection.

After my session, I feel calm, sure that all will be well. The feeling stays with me through the day. For the first time in years, I sleep through the night, so soundly that neither thoughts nor dreams interrupt my peace.

THE LIGHT FROM HERE

Surgery Day
July 13, 2012

My eyes open before the alarm goes off. It's 4:30 a.m., still dark. I seem to have forgotten what's happening today, for I am full of energy and excitement. I think it's because getting up this early usually means I'm going somewhere—on an adventure—and I'm ready.

"You awake yet?" I whisper to Tim. His lids lift in reply. I lean toward him. "Let's pretend we're going to hike Mount Katahdin today."

We have both hiked Maine's tallest mountain a couple of times, though never together, so Tim knows about the day-long hike, which begins with the Abol Trail, the fastest way up, like a boulder staircase for giants. He raises his body from bed with uncharacteristic eagerness, especially considering the hour, and grins, letting me know he plans to climb alongside me today.

Maine's license plate reads *Vacationland*, a distinction earned for the saturated, seven-week period from the Fourth of July to the end of August. Route 1, which runs through many of Maine's coastal villages, often drags with travelers and delivery trucks. The lineup of people and cars at Red's Eats lobster shack by the Wiscasset bridge can delay traffic for up to an hour.

But now, at the rim of day, the road is a smooth, unmarked ribbon. When we reach my favorite stretch near Bath, where salty inlets weave along both sides of the two-lane highway, the sky grows luminous in washes of pink and yellow. As I look out at the contours of water and sky, I notice that the spruce trees and the silver-white, rose, and indigo above the horizon are mirrored in the water below, forming one extended plane that—with Tim at my side—I feel a part of, too.

Without even trying, we make record time, arriving at Mercy Hospital in Portland at the peak of morning's glow. The hospital is a new building, four stories of brick with church-like, arched windows spanning two floors on the front side, now gilded by the sun. Dr. Molin has scheduled me first, with the intention that I'll be going home later today, but I have packed a bag because I can't imagine being released on the same day of major surgery. This is my first surgery and I have no idea what to expect.

Soon after checking in, I hear the receptionist call my name. Tim accompanies me into the prep area, where we meet Linda, the morning nurse. It's only 6:30 a.m., but she looks like she's been up for hours, bright-eyed and attentive as she suits me in a flannel-soft, lavender-colored body sac that she connects to a small heater. The contrast of the rushing warmth against the crisp cold of the surgical ward makes me giggle.

"I want one of these at *my* house."

"It's amazing, isn't it?" She smiles. "Research shows that heat improves surgery results and recovery time."

As I relax into the warmth, the anesthesiologist arrives. A quiet, serious man, he describes his protocol, ending by cautioning me not to be a martyr about pain. "Promise you'll take pain relief when offered?"

His gentle tone and protective gaze persuade me. "If you say so."

Dr. Molin breezes by with a quick wave, and Cathy, one of the two nurses in Dr. Molin's practice, enters our curtained cubicle.

"How're you doin'?" Her red hair, freckles, and slight Boston accent remind me of my Irish Catholic childhood. The crucifix hanging at the cubicle entrance seals the deal. It's as if a family member has arrived to shepherd me through the day.

"We're going to give you an injection of radioactive dye for the sentinel-node biopsy," she explains. I nod, recalling what she told me when she called earlier in the week, how the injected dye will travel into my lymphatic system to the lymph nodes closest to my tumors (called the sentinel nodes). This will indicate the path my cancer cells took if they left one of my tumors and journeyed into a lymph node.

Dr. Molin will see the dye while she's doing the surgery and remove the affected lymph node or nodes for testing, taking as many as necessary. If the sentinel nodes are free of cancer, then the cancer isn't likely to have spread, removing the need for chemo or radiation.

After I receive the injection, Cathy touches my arm reassuringly. "Now we wait. It will take about forty-five minutes for the dye to make its way to the lymph nodes. I'll be back later with some forms for you to fill out."

The initial wave of activity is complete and I'm starting to notice a few faint nerves. I remember the print I brought to soothe me, and I ask Tim to get it from my bag. Focusing on the image reminds me to breathe deeply and relax. I'm still gazing at the image when the morning nurse, Linda, returns.

"What's that?"

"It's a print of one of my paintings. I brought it to help me stay calm."

She looks more closely. "I've got three boys at home. They're still young and they wreck everything, so I don't have pretty things like this. There's no point. But still…I'd like to someday."

I nod. "I grew up with five brothers. My mom used to say she was living in a zoo."

Linda laughs, and we exchange boy tales. When she tells us how her husband joins her band of boys, outnumbering her fourfold, she shrugs her shoulders and smiles, her cheeks as flushed as a cherub's.

"I think we should give Linda a copy of this print," Tim says when Linda ducks out.

"You've read my mind. Let's make arrangements before we leave."

With Linda, Cathy, and the other hospital personnel coming and going, an hour has passed. The blue stream of dye has now journeyed through my breast and it is time. Two hefty guys arrive to lift me onto the gurney, and after a quick peck from Tim, I am headed down the long, sterile hallway, toward the double doors of the operating room.

Sunlight pours through the two-story windows of the room. The space is large and immaculate, full of machines and medical personnel—almost everything gleaming stainless or white. I am lifted onto the slender operating table and within seconds oxygen is pouring from the mask into my lungs. The anesthesiologist arrives to connect my arm to the IV and the room fades away...

I think I hear Dr. Molin's voice, and I open my eyes to see what looks like an impressionist version of her shape standing beside me.

"You're taking your time this morning," she says.

"Hhooow maaany lymppph?" I manage to ask.

"I only took a couple. Everything went well."

I wake up intermittently, like a hung-over teenager sleeping in on the weekend. Eventually, hunger drives me upright and I ask the young nurse if I am allowed to eat.

"Sure. But first, would you like another dose of painkillers? You're allowed one more."

I don't feel any pain, but I recall what the anesthesiologist told me about not trying to tough it out. I'm too fuzzy headed to remember that I'm extremely sensitive to meds, so I say, "Sure, I guess."

She hands me the cooler of food that Tim gave her, and I start nibbling on the rice salad with chicken and vegetables I brought. The garlic dressing tastes much better going down than coming back up minutes later. *Ugh, I shouldn't have had that last dose of meds. I wish my head would stop spinning. I think I'm going to throw up again.*

"You were in recovery forever," Tim is telling me. "It seemed like everyone else came out before you, and you went in first." He has my right hand in his, held tight, and is gently stroking my forearm. "I've gotta tell you, I was nervous."

"How do you feel now?" Cathy asks, unwrapping the blood pressure band from my right arm. "Your blood pressure is still pretty low."

"Weak…hungry…I want to eat, but please, nothing with garlic."

"Her blood pressure runs low," Tim says, "and she's been known to pass out from hunger."

"I can get you something from the hospital kitchen," Cathy offers. "Do you like oatmeal?" Tim and I smile in reply, as this is my breakfast six days out of seven. "Yes, please."

Two helpings later, I'm starting to see straight. "Wow, I feel so much better now."

"You're getting your color back, and your blood pressure is better, too." Cathy smiles. "You had me worried there."

"How many lymph nodes did Dr. Molin take?" I ask. "How did they look?"

"Everything went well. She said things looked good. I'm not sure how many she took."

"I think I heard her say 'a couple,' but I was in such a daze. Do I have a drain?"

"No drain. If we can get you strong enough, we'll send you home this afternoon."

"I'm not ready. I feel so weak."

Hours pass. The second shift arrives, including Dr. Molin's afternoon nurse, Elisabeth. She and the ward nurse who covers the second shift are on a mission to move me out of my cubicle. They keep trying to get me up, but I'm still groggy, so whenever they ask me if I am ready, I say, "Not yet."

At 3 p.m., shortly after a two-escort trip to the bathroom, I find my strength and tell them I think I'll be okay to go home. I'm worried about the weekend traffic on Route 1 and the long backup at the Wiscasset bridge. I don't want to be stuck in a car with an aching chest. But by some miracle, there is no traffic this Friday, and we sail along almost as easily as we did in the morning.

I am so thrilled with the day's success that I make a call from the passenger seat. Tim has notified family, but I want to let Gloria know how I'm doing.

"I'm on my way home," I tell her. "Everything went well. I just wanted to thank you for your help yesterday. I slept through the night. Can you believe it? I'm giving you the credit."

"No, I can't believe it. I can't believe I'm talking to you just hours after your surgery."

At my favorite part of the drive, the halfway mark in Bath, the sun is nearing the edge of its arc, reigning over fields, waterways, and white clapboard farmhouses as we pass. By the time we reach home, the glow is peaking, turning Emily into a beam of light as she runs to the car to meet us. Cole joins her and they walk me to the porch, where we sit and steep in the warmth of the remaining day.

THE LIGHT FROM HERE

Rest
Mid to Late July 2012

Before my surgery I fashioned a bed on the shady side of our porch. I made it by facing two large wicker chairs toward each other and adding an ottoman in between so it would fit my length. Like a bird making her nest I kept adding things—a down comforter, pillows, a sheepskin, coverlets—hovering near my creation until it was just right.

At the time, I wasn't sure how much I'd use it, but in the first few days after my surgery, I find myself lying in it much of the day, hazily rolling in and out of sleep. Discomfort is easily managed with a few over-the-counter pain meds, leaving me free to merge with the gentle breathing of summer. The smell of sweet alyssum wafts by. A woodpecker taps rhythmically in my dreams.

Nourishment arrives whenever I need it, brought by a hive of makers who take turns bringing home-cooked meals. Emily often serves me on the porch. She arranges the tray, uses my favorite mug, and includes a sprig of nasturtium in a tiny vase. Her voice is soothing as she asks if there is anything else I'd like.

My mother, who so thoroughly wired me for guilt, also—quite unknowingly—prepared me to accept this attention.

"You can't imagine it," she told me years ago, her voice uncharacteristically excited. "Every evening, a meal arrives, a full meal, you know, meat, potatoes, vegetables, bread—even dessert—and it's so delicious, like last night we had a scrumptious casserole with chicken in cream sauce, and an apple pie for dessert, and it was heavenly. And then *your father* does the dishes! He's so delighted with the meals and all the treats, and he knows *I* can't do anything with my broken collarbone and wrist, so he gets up and he does them, just like that. I tell you, he's been a saint!"

I didn't recognize the person on the other end of the line. Hadn't my mother just experienced the worst accident of her life? And here she was, sounding as happy as I'd ever heard her.

This was deep medicine—I knew it even then—and now I see that it is my turn to follow my mother's example. People want to be kind, and if I accept their offerings graciously, I grant them the fullness of their actions. My efforts might even loosen my deeply seated belief that there isn't enough to go around.

"Wow," I say to my neighbor Sarah, "look at this! Indian food, you say? Tell me about it."

She grins as she places the brown grocery bags on our kitchen counter. "It's one of our family's favorite meals. I made sure to bring *poppadoms* and chutney, too. They're the best part."

"This is wonderful, Sarah. Such a treat! And you brought more than a meal's worth. How did you know I love having leftovers for lunch?"

Five days into my recovery, it's time to hear the pathology report. Tim drives me to Portland for the follow-up with Dr. Molin on a clear August day.

I imagine my left breast as a specimen, separate from me, providing tissue samples but nothing more—no sexiness, sustenance, or sensation. I picture the technician whose job it is to dissect what was once my holy ground, extracting the two small tumors and slicing them into slivers for the lab. I picture the pathologist gazing into the microscope, studying the slide. I ask Tim, "Do you think the pathologist ever wonders about the women behind the cells? I would."

We arrive at Dr. Molin's, and as usual, we don't wait long. Once in the examining room she gets right to it. "I'm sorry to tell you I don't have the news we wanted to hear. There was a tiny nick of cancer in your lymph node, a two-millimeter bump on the exterior, about the size of a small pimple." She stops and makes eye contact with me, then Tim.

"If all had gone as I had anticipated, you'd have no further active treatment, but this little bump changes things."

"How so?" Tim asks.

"I'm a surgeon, not an oncologist, but the normal course of treatment when there is cancer in a lymph node or nodes is four to six rounds of chemotherapy three weeks apart, then a month break, then six weeks of radiation." She doesn't go into detail, preferring we get the facts from a medical oncologist and a radiation oncologist, both trained for the next legs of the journey.

When Dr. Molin uses the difficult cancer words, her voice stays level, as if she is saying "six cups of flour" instead of "six rounds of chemo." Her directness and calm keep the associations of those words at a safe distance for now. She answers a few questions from Tim, but I'm unable to focus on their exchange.

Dr. Molin turns to me and says, "Let's take a look at your incision." She helps me onto the examining table and unwraps my bandage.

"It looks good. How does it feel?"

"I'm still getting used to it. There isn't much pain—it's more numb than anything. When it gets sore I take a couple of Tylenol and that really helps."

"That's good. Do you have any questions?"

The question that's been gnawing at my stomach ever since I heard Dr. Molin say *cancer in the lymph node* is the question I'm afraid to ask. But I make myself do it. "Dr. Molin, do you think…well…did we wait too long to do the surgery?"

Her eyes, as precise as her scalpel, penetrate me with her reply. "Blaming won't change anything now."

She is right. I chose Dr. Molin in part because she supported me in my desire to have the surgery after my art opening. We will never know when that nick of cancer entered my lymph node. Stewing over it now will not take it away.

"Truthfully, Maureen, I don't believe the wait made a difference," she says, her voice calm and convincing. "Now sit tight and Cathy will be right along to finish up."

"How're you doin'?" Cathy asks, lifting her blue gaze toward mine.

"Did you hear about my results?"

She nods, her fingers moving tenderly across the swollen areas near the incision. Earlier in the day, I took my first peek, knowing what was coming. Now I give my puffy red scar another quick glance. I'm not ready for a long stare.

"You're healing nicely, but we need to keep an eye on this spot," she says as she presses a small swollen area at the beginning of the incision. "Some fluids are pooling here, but that's normal. Your body is trying to reabsorb all the fluids that collected after your surgery."

She begins the process of re-wrapping my torso with a bandeau-style ace bandage.

"Can you tell me about your work?"

"I'm an artist and I also have several people that I help, all but one of them elderly."

"Oh, that's nice. How do you help them?"

"I do all kinds of things—pay bills, bring them to appointments, provide companionship. I thought I'd start back to work next week. They need me, you know."

Cathy's face grows concerned. "Hmm…I understand, but I'd like to see you take more time before you do anything too physical, including driving. Your body has been through a lot, you know."

"I guess it has."

"Cathy knows what she's talking about," Tim says. "We'll pick up the slack."

Cathy smiles at Tim, then me. "You have a nice family. You're lucky."

"I know. They've been so good."

"Well, then, it's settled. No driving, lifting, or reaching for another couple of weeks. Try to rest as much as you can, okay?"

I nod. "With your permission."

"Good Maureen, I'll see you again when you come back at the end of next week for your oncology appointment. Just take it easy."

I send an e-mail to family members and friends:

Well, the news was not what we had hoped for. There was a small amount of cancer in my lymph node. So it's back to information gath-

ering. Next week we will meet with two oncologists and hear what course of treatment they recommend.

I'm not surprised by this news. It's as if I knew all along, but was still hopeful. So I'm not too crushed right now, just soggy. It is hard to muster your strength when you are still recovering from surgery. But I will, in time.

The last thing Dr. Molin said to me, looking me straight in the eye, was, "This is curable. This is curable."

So please keep me in your thoughts and prayers. It really helps, knowing I am being lifted by your collective strength, which right now is much larger than my own.

With gratitude,

Maureen

The Fight
July 27, 2012

Tim is driving me home from back-to-back appointments, first with Dr. Molin, then with the oncologist at Mercy Hospital, a gentle man who told us about a test I qualify for that determines the merit of chemo, in terms of protection from recurrence. Research has shown that for certain types of breast cancer patients, chemotherapy offers no significant improvement in long-term survival.

The sky is clear today, the air salty. It's the kind of summer weather I usually relish, but I can't get comfortable in the bucket seat of our ten-year-old Honda. My wound smarts and my left arm aches. I have to sit tilted to the right, with the cotton pillow that the nurses sent me home with after my surgery tucked between my arm and my missing breast. It's a pathetic little pillow, under stuffed and garishly green, but some sweet soul from the local survivor's club made it by hand and by now it has become like a blankie to me. I don't go anywhere without it.

"I still can't believe I may not have to have chemo. I almost don't dare hope. I don't see how I could survive the nausea. And my hair—"

"I bet you won't have to," Tim cuts in. "I just have a feeling."

What do you know, I say to myself. *You're just trying to make me feel better.* I adjust my position again, still trying to get comfortable.

I think about the handout I was given at my first appointment with Dr. Molin. My heart dropped when I read a passage explaining that, after diagnosis, it was important to express the full range of one's feelings, including the tough ones. Reading this made me wonder if my two years of anxiety and stress had contributed to my getting cancer. The handout wasn't worded in a blaming way but I felt so implicated that I hid it away. Still, its message crept into my thoughts each time I held back from expressing my true feelings with Tim. An exchange we had when I was preparing for my art show was particularly hurtful. I asked him to post a notice about my show on his Facebook page, and to my surprise, he refused, saying he didn't think Facebook was for promoting one's business.

When I questioned this, giving examples of artist friends who post information on their shows, he didn't bend. His stern stance made me think he didn't want people to associate *my* art with *him*, an insecurity I'd been carrying since shifting from realistic to symbolic painting.

"You don't like my art, that's it," I said.

"That's not it at all," he countered. "I just don't feel comfortable using Facebook for business purposes. I don't think it's appropriate."

"I disagree. I'm your wife. People won't think you're taking advantage. They'll think you're being a supportive husband."

I was shocked and shaken that he wouldn't do what I asked, especially knowing what I was going through. But he had been so good about everything else that I forced myself to turn away from our disagreement that day, not wanting to confront all the uncertainties that arose from the interaction.

Through the weeks of surgery and recovery, each time I remembered the scene, I felt an uncomfortable mix of sadness and anger.

Now I decide I need to follow the advice of the handout and speak up.

"There's something I want to let you know," I begin. "Um...well...this might seem strange, but I'm still upset that you didn't post my show opening on your Facebook page last month. I've tried to let it go but it keeps coming up and it keeps hurting, and—"

"What?" Tim interrupts, the "t" sounding somewhat like a slap.

"Don't you remember? You refused to post my show announcement."

His brown eyes, usually warm and soft, begin to narrow. He sighs forcefully and says, "You didn't ask me to post your show announcement. We talked about it. That's all."

"I *did* ask you to post it. We talked about it for quite a while, and you disagreed with me. And why are you getting so defensive? I'm just trying to let you know how I feel."

He glances at me, eyebrows furrowing. "You haven't been listening to me. I just don't think Facebook is for promoting yourself."

"I know; that's what you told me before. But I'm not some random business. I'm your wife and I only have one show a year." My voice falters. "Say what you like, but my cousin posted my art opening on *her* Facebook page without even being asked. She even commented that she was proud of me."

"What?" Another slapping "t." "You don't think I'm proud of you?"

"I'm not saying that, but I know you're not crazy about my paintings and I think the reason you didn't post my opening is that you're a little embarrassed to be associated with them." I remind him that he used to compliment my paintings, but rarely does anymore. "I know it's not in the marriage contract to fake a feeling you don't have, but this is different. You should know me well enough to know how much I need your support during this period."

"You think I'm not supporting you?" He practically growls, eyes darkened, anger sharpening his words into barbs that shoot out in hisses with short pauses in between. "You...oh...God...this is...so...frustrating."

I burst into tears. "Why are you getting so mad? You're not listening to me!" I'm choking on sobs, sputtering sentences. "Can't you tell what I'm trying to say? This hurts! You're being mean! Can't you see that?"

"WHAT DO YOU THINK I AM, A FUCKING MIND READER?"

This yanks me out of my pain. Tim gets angry only when he is brought to the brink, and he almost never swears. *It's true. I want him to read my mind—to know me so well that I don't have to explain what I need.*

I look at him, his tanned face reddened by passion, and I feel a strange mix of compassion and regret. Strangely, I also feel almost excited that we are having a real fight—one of a very small handful in our twenty-eight years together.

"You're right," I say. I wait in silence. "I want you to read my mind, and that's not fair." I wait again. "I didn't mean to hurt you. I just thought you should know how I feel. I didn't realize it would be such a bomb." I keep staring at him, surprised at how much better, how much lighter I feel now that I've spoken.

My mood can switch in an instant, but Tim is not like me. I notice his brow, still tense.

"Are you okay?"

"Not really," he says, and stays quiet for the rest of the drive.

E-mail, July 28:

> *Dear Friends and Family,*
>
> *Hello from my favorite location these days, my front porch. I am unable to drive or pick up anything weighing more than a pound, so I have relinquished the usual summer flurry in place of restful observation. Some of my favorite scenes:*
>
> *Tim's rustle in the veggie beds, picking beans, harvesting garlic...*

A pair of goldfinch, flitting from leaf to branch, chasing each other like a couple of teenagers in love.

Pollen-heavy bumblebees, scouring the salvia for more.

And, in between, we have met two oncologists who both recommend a test that will determine what I'm calling "the personality" of my cells. If my score is low, chemo will not be necessary; high and it will. So, again, we will wait, this time for a little over a week. I am healing well, albeit slowly, from the surgery, and there are no concerns there.

It is so nice to have you with me on this journey. I am full of gratitude and, in this moment, smiling with your love.

Best to all,

Maureen

THE LIGHT FROM HERE

Slow Healing

August 1 to August 10, 2012

E-mail, August 8:

Warmth surrounds me right now...a sleeping dog on one side...a doting daughter on the other. The breeze carries birdsong, bee hum, and the rumble of the neighbor's mower. The fullness of summer is filling me completely.

Last week brought predictable "bumps" in my journey: pain, immobility, fear of what may come. Perhaps the grace that had lifted me for the last two months set me down so that I could experience gravity, at least for a spell.

We met the radiation oncologist, who recommended thirty-three radiation treatments, which translates to about six-and-a-half weeks of daily (weekday) treatments. These will commence in a couple of weeks if I don't have chemo. If I do have chemo, they will begin a month after I finish it, sometime next winter.

We thought we would find out today about the results of my test to determine whether chemo is warranted, but we haven't. My oncologist sent two tissue samples. The results of the first sample caused her to order that they run the second sample (not sure why) so guess what? We must wait another week.

But I must say that I feel so calm today that I'm glad for this. It means another week to heal, to breathe in the perfection of this summer, to stretch my heart around all the love coming my way. It's a true cascade and it's much more powerful than any of the above-mentioned trials.

Thank you for all the ways you are easing these days for me. My gratitude is bursting!

Much love,

Maureen

I'm standing in front of our bathroom sink, taking my morning sponge bath, dabbing a wet washcloth down my pale limbs and frame. I turn to face Tim, still damp from his shower, and he begins our twice-daily ritual, unfastening the end of the wrap encasing my chest and holding it while I turn to unravel the stretchy fabric. I always end facing away from the mirror, where I close my eyes and wait for Tim to take a look. In another setting, this scene might be steamy, but there are no strands of sensuality here.

"It's looking good," Tim says. "Would you like to see?"

"No. Just wrap me back up nice and tight. It feels better that way."

He starts winding the band around my chest again.

"You're healing well."

"I don't know. My armpit feels like it's been nipped and tied. Every time I try to lift my arm above my chest it says nope, no go. It's been almost three weeks and I thought I'd be driving by now, but I wouldn't feel safe if I had to make a quick turn. My left side is still weak."

"Don't rush it. One of us can drive you to work."

"The hardest part is not being able to go for a walk. You know how important that is for me. But every step pulls on my incision, and the pain gets worse as I go on." I let out a long sigh. "It's just so frustrating."

"Remember what Cathy said about taking it easy." Tim fastens the fabric. "You just had major surgery. You need to give it time."

"My radiation doctor said I should start swimming to get my arm moving. She showed me the radiation position, with my arms bent behind my head, and she said that swimming would be good therapy to help with range of motion." I try to show Tim the position, but can only reach halfway up. "I can't imagine going swimming right now or putting my arms up like that."

Tim looks concerned. "What do you think could help?"

"I start physical therapy next week, so hopefully that will do something.

Cathy told me that there's a special therapy, just for mastectomy patients, and that Dr. Molin's office petitioned the insurance companies in Maine to cover it. I tell you, those women are my heroes."

"Mine, too." Tim nods as he helps me get my shirt over my head.

It's been almost a week since our fight, and as I hoped, we have eased back to normal. No—we're better. Tim is leaning in more, looking at me more frequently and tenderly. He is trying, and I feel it.

"I think we should fight more often," I tell him when I'm sure we're past the aftershocks.

He looks puzzled, his brows furrowing in reply. "I don't think so."

"No, really. I feel so much better. Every once in a while, I've got to let my red out, you know." I growl and lean to hug him. He recoils playfully and I drag my fingers down the front of his shirt, ending with an embrace.

This time he accepts, lifting me off the ground and giving an ample squeeze. He sets me down and asks, "When do you think we will hear the test results?"

"I'm not exactly sure. Probably sometime next week—while you're away."

"I have a good feeling. I think they ran the second test because the results of the first were good, and they just want to make sure."

"Really?"

"Think about it. If the first test indicated you needed chemo, why would they bother with the second one? Aren't they $9,000 each?"

"I get your logic. You're probably right, but I don't want to latch on. I'd be crushed if we got the call and were wrong. Better to stay neutral."

But the wheels of hope are turning. When I survey the garden from the porch each morning, the hydrangeas seem to be cheering me on.

Tim is leaving for Wyoming in a few days and I'm glad for it. He has been attending appointments, washing dishes, paying medical bills, and bearing my emotional waves for almost three months, and I think we're both ready for some space. I would say a break, but there won't be much rest on this trip; a National Outdoor Leadership School (NOLS) graduate, he will be on a service project in backcountry Wyoming, rebuilding a trail bridge with hand tools and brute strength.

I have been urging him for a couple of years to do something like this, to follow his nose toward something new. He signed up for the trip back in February, nearly thirty years after his three-month-long semester in the Rockies with NOLS. When I was diagnosed in June, he was all set to cancel, but I convinced him to keep the plan, especially once we knew that the timing was during a lull between treatments. I was originally excited for a week on my own, and though my current situation doesn't mirror what I envisioned, I am still glad for the break.

I've got a project to sink into while he is gone, too. Our twenty-fifth wedding anniversary is coming in a month and I have ordered an antique-style, wooden cubby unit for a blank wall in our kitchen, a space that Tim regularly points to and says, "It's been eight years. When are we going to put something here?"

I have been eyeing this piece for a while, and I'm finally ready to buy it, especially since I've noticed that it has twenty-five compartments, one for each year of our union. While Tim is away, I plan to scour every shoebox, album, and digital file for photos of our time together, choosing the best one from each year. I have one month to search, locate, and make copies of the pictures, which I will tape inside the cubbies when I present the gift.

While envisioning all of this, I am reminding myself that my unsentimental husband will probably not be presenting me with something similarly special. If I were wise, I would picture that the present is for both of us. Still, I cling to a thread of hope that he will surprise me somehow, especially given the circumstances.

On the morning before Tim leaves, we're in our bathroom together, doing our morning routine. Tomorrow, Tim will not be here to help me so I want to prepare myself. At the end of the unwrapping, I open my eyes, turn toward the mirror, and stare.

"It looks so weird," I say, disturbed by the asymmetry before me.

"I think it's a cool scar," Tim says. "I love it."

"I thought I would too, but right now I don't. I'd rather be looking at a breast than this puffy red squiggle." A few tears roll out. I take in a full breath and sigh. "I guess I'll get used to it." I touch the skin above and below the incision, prodding tentatively.

"Do you feel anything?" Tim asks.

"No, it's strange…numb…like it's not part of my body." My gaze slides back and forth from mirror to skin, surveying my body as if it were a new landscape.

"Time to bind me back up. Isn't it strange that after all these years of not wearing a bra, hating the feeling of constriction, now I want this thing wrapped tight around my chest. I'm uncomfortable without it."

Tim adeptly performs the re-wrapping. He's got the tension perfectly and I can tell by his expression that he is enjoying having mastered this skill.

That evening, our last night together for ten days, Tim unwraps me once again, holding the fabric while I turn, this time in near darkness. We haven't made love since before my surgery, and I know Tim is waiting for my lead. He'll be gone for a while and I'd like to connect physically before he goes. I have felt his tenderness since recovering from our fight—as if a barrier has been removed.

I'm not sure I'm physically ready for this, but my heart wants to try.

At the end of the unraveling, I lift my good arm to the curve behind his neck, reach my lips to his, and give him a sustained kiss to let him know it's time.

"Are you sure?" he asks.

In reply, I pull his head down and lean back to receive a second kiss, this time to my right breast. I grab his arm, squeeze it tightly and lead him to our bed, where we kiss into a blur, skin pulsing with the pleasure and relief for our bodies to be loving again. My right breast tingles and surges, sending messages to the rest of my cells, reeling in an expanse of ecstasy.

I kept my breast and I'm so glad that it's mine, that it's mine to feel.

THE LIGHT FROM HERE

Waiting with the Monarch

August 10 to August 30, 2012

E-mails, August 14:

Dear Ones,

I just heard from my oncologist that BOTH of my scores were low, which means that I WON'T have chemo!!!!!!!!!

I wish you could see my smile right now :-)))))))

Thanks again for all your support!

Big love,

Maureen

Dear Maureen,

Oh, what wonderful news! I'm so excited I can't even type—that last sentence took me five tries (or "tires," as I just wrote)!

Good, good news. Take care,

Love, M

YIPPPPPPEEEEEEEEE! I AM SOOOOOOOOOO EXCITED!!!!!!!!!!!!! AND JOYFULLLLLLLL!!!!!!!!

I will be over later with soup and salad. You can have tonight or freeze for a colder day!!

K

"Mommy, look what I've got!" Emily is a wide-eyed twenty going on six as she holds up a glass jar, stuffed so full of milkweed leaves that I must search to locate the yellow, black, and white striped caterpillar. I know it's there because this was once our family's ritual; each summer we would scour the milkweed field by our former house to find a monarch caterpillar, bring it home, and see it through its stages of change.

"It's so tiny," I say, "but not for long."

In the days that follow, our kitchen island becomes a monarch hub, magnetizing our family to the eating, the growing, and the resting, while the little guy eats roughly 3,000 times its body weight in milkweed, a plant poisonous to most other animals.

"We'll need to keep the jar well stocked," I say to Emily. "Our friend is *hungry*."

"I'll be at the farm today," she says. "I'll get more milkweed then."

I never fully noticed the details of the monarch's transitions in the past, when raising my family corralled most of my attention. Now I am riveted, growing more observant of the micro steps, watching for each stage, and trying to be present for the moments of change.

One afternoon, I am in the kitchen alone, and a bit of movement from the jar catches my eye. It's been a few days since the caterpillar reached full size and began her restless phase, inching around the inside of the jar looking for something to attach to. I put a stick inside, which she eventually bonded to, then moved into J-formation, where she remained for a day.

Now her slender tube has uncurled, and her body is expanding and contracting, moving up and down and in and out, writhing and squirming like Houdini trying to wriggle out of a straightjacket. She shakes rapid-fire for minutes to slough off the papery sheath—now a crumpled black bit. One last round of convulsing expels the skin to reveal a shape-changing, small, green orb, still pulsing and jerking, rippling in and out. Minutes pass, its movement slows, and the form grows more compact, settling at last into an elongated sphere just over an inch long, wider at the top. It looks like a smooth, shining piece of jade with a ridge of dots that shimmer like gold leaf, and one black spot on either side, perfectly symmetrical—as elegant as a piece of jewelry. I stare at it each time I am near.

I am not able to talk to Tim during his time in the wilderness, so when word comes that both of my test scores are low enough to avoid having chemo, I call the NOLS office to see if they can reach him.

"I have some very important news to share with my husband," I tell the man at the desk. "I know they don't have cell coverage, but surely you must have a way to communicate with the group."

"Actually ma'am, we do not."

"But this is very important. I have cancer, and I just found out that I don't have to have chemotherapy. I want my husband to know so he won't be worrying."

"Well, now that I think of it," the man says, "Glenn from the staff is joining the group later in the week. If you e-mail me your message, I will print it and put it in a sealed envelope for him to deliver to your husband."

"Oh thank you. That will be perfect."

Our monarch fairy tale is nearing its end, an enchantment that has held our family during the weeks of my coming back to strength. Yesterday, the chrysalis went black, signifying its final phase of metamorphosis. Butterflies wait for warm air before they release from their cocoons. In late August in Maine, that means daytime, and I'm ready, placing the chrysalis into the first patch of sunlight on the porch before I start my morning vigil, breakfast in hand. I'll be leaving for work in two hours and I'm hoping to witness the birth before I go.

As I stare at the chrysalis, its solid black color gradually begins to reveal geometric shapes and the telltale orange. These are the wings, folded in tightly, waiting for the cocoon—now a thin, clear skin—to split apart.

Emily, still groggy with sleep, tiptoes outside to join me. She stands behind me, stroking my hair for a while before sitting on the opposite side of the chrysalis, facing me. She looks up and we smile at each other—butterfly kin.

We slip into the silence of attentive waiting.

The birth happens in slow motion, as the translucent skin tears to release the butterfly. Her wings are damp, highlighted with flecks of white, and her body is pulsing, plump with food stored to last through her first day.

We stay with her as long as we can before setting off to work. We hate to leave.

When I return hours later the butterfly is still on the porch. She is perfectly formed now—body slender, wings dry—poised on the table by our front door. Just as I reach her, she lifts off and nearly brushes past my cheek. She lands nearby, choosing the long, purple spire of the buddleia bush for her first meal. Her black feeding straw unfurls and reaches into the tiny flowers of one of the panicles to drink its nectar. She touches down on a few more spires, then moves away.

I stand on the edge of the porch watching her land and take off until, at last, she disappears from view. Her departure stirs me. She has trained me to *her* cycles, contented to be home, slowed to *her* pace. I'm not sure I'm ready to end this phase or if I'm prepared for what comes next.

THE LIGHT FROM HERE

Preparing for Radiation
August 31 to September 3, 2012

"Did you know you missed your appointment?" It's a woman's voice, slightly abrupt, on the other end of the line.

"My appointment is at three o'clock," I say, fumbling through the pile of cards by the phone to make sure I'm right.

"No. You were scheduled for ten-thirty, over half an hour ago. Can you come now?"

"I live an hour away. I'm not ready."

The woman is insistent.

"I'll try to get there by two."

"We'll just have to fit you in somehow," the voice says, still curt. "Come as soon as you can."

Until now I was not expecting this appointment to be stressful. I gave Tim, who has attended most of my doctor's visits, the day off from accompanying me.

"They call it a dry run," I told him when he offered. "They're just going to set up the machine for my radiation mapping. It should be no big deal."

So I drive myself. When I arrive at the radiation treatment center, the reception room is empty and the lights behind the reception desk are off as if the office is closed. I wait for a minute but no one comes, so I follow a small hallway to a second room, which is larger and full of people, half of them wearing johnnies. No one acknowledges me. Most are older men with blank faces. No one looks happy.

I return to the empty room and stand by the reception window for minutes, praying that someone will show up to greet me. No one does. I have no choice but to return to the bigger room, clear my throat and say, "This is my first time. Can someone tell me what to do?"

A middle-aged woman dressed in street clothes points to the hallway and says, "Change into a johnny in one of those dressing rooms and wait here until you're called."

Ugh...johnnies. They are always too big for me. Well, at least they've got robes, too. I wrap one over the johnny so that I'm encased down to my calves.

I return to the waiting room and take a corner seat by an end table piled with magazines. After about fifteen minutes, a young woman appears and calls a name—not mine. She looks harried and does not acknowledge me, so I resolve to take action when she returns. Another fifteen minutes passes and this time I rush toward her when she enters the room.

I give her my name and let her know that no one was there to check me in when I arrived.

"We're understaffed today," the woman says. "We'll get to you after we finish with everyone else. You may have to wait a while."

I return to my seat and scan the room to count the other cotton-robed people—four. I'm glad for the tall stack of magazines because I figure I've got at least another hour to wait.

In between *Martha Stewart* and *Coastal Living*, I smile at anyone willing to make eye contact. One woman tells me that we usually don't wait this long. There must be a problem. Later I hear that the machine is having a bad day and so are the staff. It's the Friday before Labor Day and the technicians have been working since 6:30 this morning, over nine hours ago.

When it's my turn, I decide to be cheerful to help them get through their last procedure before their holiday weekend. I smile at all four of the technicians as I enter the room and say, "Last one, right?"

A tall, pretty brunette with expressive brown eyes is the only one to respond. "So sorry to keep you waiting this long. We usually run a pretty tight ship around here and you normally will be in and out in fifteen minutes." She approaches me, introduces herself as Dawn, and explains that today will take longer because they will be programming the machine for my treatment plan.

The room is large and windowless, dominated by a monster-sized metal machine in the center. A shallow-domed hood, like a small spaceship, looms over a long, metal bench with rows of two-inch holes in straight lines. The space is cold and dark, with a few spotlights shining on the machine. To me, the bands of eerie light conjure torture scenes from *Batman*, a series I watched with my brothers as a child.

Dawn asks me to remove my robe. She lays a pillowcase over the holes on the bench and directs me to lie on it, slip my arms out of the johnny, and raise them into the armrests overhead.

"I'm sorry it's so chilly in here," she says. "Would you like heated sheets?"

I am trying to be easy on them, so I decline. I'm more concerned about my arms: when I stretch them above my head my left shoulder is uncomfortably tight. Now I understand why the radiation doctor encouraged me to swim and stretch my arms to prepare for the radiation position. *I wish I had done more.*

One of the other technicians, a thin-lipped blonde, older and more serious than the others, gives instructions, rattling off numbers and technical phrases foreign to me. I close my eyes and try to relax. The minutes tick by. My shoulder discomfort is joined by a sharp pain in my upper back where the edge of one of the circular cutouts in the bench is pressing into my shoulder blade. I curse myself for not having taken the offer of warm sheets; the cold air makes it impossible to relax.

I'm starting to falter. I want to be resilient, but the sequence of the last few hours has stripped me—now quite literally—of my warmth and calm. The pain gets worse until my discomfort turns to anger. I can't get past the growing feeling of being tortured, especially since I've now been abandoned by the technicians, who are directing the machine's movements from a protected booth away from my sight. I squeeze my eyes tightly to hold back tears, but they are leaking out, rolling down the sides of my face, adding an annoying itch to my other ills. I have been told by the stern woman that I cannot, under any circumstances, move, and I've never wished to do so more in my life.

How long has it been? I wish they would talk to me, tell me we're almost done. I can't stand another moment of this. Minutes pass. I'm trying to keep my chest from jiggling, but the sobs are pressing for release.

At last I sense a body nearby and open my eyes to see Dawn, who smiles and says, "You did a great job, Maureen. That took much longer than normal because we had to set everything up. Thank you for your patience."

I fling my arms out of their traps and wrap the johnny snugly around my chest. I am so relieved that the ordeal is over that I'm suddenly cheerful, wishing them all a good weekend as I leave, glad to know I have three whole days before I must return.

After the dry run fiasco I resolve to stay positive and not let anger take hold, but my head keeps filling with ammunition.

I don't like how they are doing this. I'm not ready to re-enter treatment and now they want to put my body through six-and-a-half weeks of stress. I don't know if I'm strong enough to get through this.

The next morning is Sunday, two days before the start of my radiation marathon. I don't want to begin already defeated, so I try to figure out how to change my attitude. An idea comes: I remember my art show guestbook filled with comments left by visitors to my past shows. I turn to it, hoping it will lift my mood.

I read through the entire book, ending at the section from my most recent show. One comment stands out. "Do you know about the naïve painters? I think you may enjoy them!" In minutes I am scrolling through the images provided by a Google search. My eye lands on a painting by Henri Rousseau called *The Dream*.

"I'm that woman!" I say out loud. *At least, I want to be that woman.*

She is nude, reclining on a velvet couch in the jungle, surrounded by lush plants and nearly hidden animals: lions, an elephant, a snake. Her skin glows, and despite the potential for danger, she looks serene.

"Look, Tim. This woman is me in the radiation pose, except she is so much calmer, of course. But it could be me."

We study the painting together. The more I look, the more I see how it fits. The woman is naked and vulnerable, surrounded by potential threats, but she is unfazed.

"Look at how elegant she is. Man, I could use some of her attitude. Will you print me a copy?"

Tim smiles approvingly. "Consider it done."

I love how Tim is so good at doing things, but at this moment he's doing something else that I don't get from him as much as I'd like. He's fixing his eyes on me, and they're warming until our joint rush can't be contained. I leap into his arms for a sustained, exuberant hug.

THE LIGHT FROM HERE

First Week of Radiation
September 4 to 7, 2012 • Radiation day 1 to day 4

Tim drives me to my first official radiation session. I stare at the print of the Rousseau painting on the way to the center—fixing my gaze on the woman in the scene. Even in the jungle, she's got her shit on. And that's the thing. She doesn't have anything on; not a stitch. And it's not safe out there. Two lions are eyeing her—the females, the hunters—they could devour her in an instant. Tear her to shreds. But she is fearless, taming the beasts, extending her arm to show them that she is their queen. They will protect and defend her with their lives. I try to imagine having her strength.

At the treatment center, I change, and this time my bottom has barely warmed the seat before I'm called in. Dawn, my brown-eyed beauty, is there again, smiling so large that you would think she was delivering my brand-new infant into my arms. But she has other plans for my upper appendages. I must lie on that hard, holey bench again, slip off the johnny, and stretch my bare twigs overhead. The left side is brittle, stiff, like a branch in winter. It doesn't have the reach.

"It was really uncomfortable last time," I tell Dawn. "I felt the metal edges cutting into me. Is there a way to pad it somehow?"

Dawn's eyes grow sympathetically larger. She rushes to get an extra pillowcase and is spreading it over the metal holes when Ms. Fussy strides in with her arm pointing to the bench. "You can't put that there," she says with pursed lips, her eyes glaring at Dawn. "Take it away."

"But she needs more padding," Dawn explains. I nod entreatingly. Ms. Fussy shakes her head at Dawn and says curtly, "Take it away. It can't stay." Dawn does as she asks. She has no choice.

In this well of defeat, I feel the edges more acutely. As the minutes pass and the enormous hood rotates overhead, beeping and whirring, I swear that the metal is slicing my skin, pressing like a dull knife trying to cut and using the brute force of my weight digging in.

I'm sick to my stomach on the ride home, weighted by the road ahead, unable to draw from the image on the card. Now the jungle looks threatening, the woman ridiculous.

Emily drives me on day two. I don't want to fall apart near her, so I strain to keep positive. The other patients in the waiting room are older men, slumped, pale, unresponsive. During my treatment, I fight back tears at the searing pain in my shoulder. The minutes are interminable.

After radiation, I'm due at Elinor's, where I work as her personal assistant once a week. Elinor has been leaving gifts on my desk—an orchid, nice soap, pretty cards—ever since my diagnosis, and I'm sure she'll be sympathetic. I'm relieved to be near someone who will understand, a sister in the breast cancer club she joined long before me.

She greets me eagerly. "How did your first two sessions go?"

"They were really hard," I say, telling her about the holes in the table, the pain in my shoulder, and the unfriendly woman in charge of the treatments. I notice that while I'm talking, Elinor is backing away from me.

"I felt nauseated afterward," I say, "kind of light-headed and—"

"No you didn't." She cuts me off.

"I did. I felt so weird and spacy."

"No, no," she shakes her head, "it's all in your mind." She laughs teasingly and swipes her hand through the air. "You're going to be fine."

I look away, incredulous. My breath is trapped in my throat. I don't have the strength to defend myself.

Elinor leaves after lunch for an appointment, and I finish my work, desolate. On my way out, I stop to talk to her handyman, Michael, who is a retired educator—kind, book-smart, and clever with his hands. He is an obsessive problem solver and when he hears about my queasy stomach he runs out to his van to fetch a roll of peppermint Tums.

"I've got a bad stomach," he says. "These work great."

"I'm not going to take them from you, Michael, but you are so nice to offer."

He plants them in my hand with an empathetic smile. "I insist."

As I'm driving down the hill of Elinor's cul-de-sac, I see her Saab approaching. I hope to pass her with only a wave, but she stops her car and lowers the window, clearly ready to speak.

"I get it," she says, her face softer than before, her eyes present, her voice wavering with emotion. "You want this to be over, but that won't happen…not ever, really. This is part of you now. But that's okay because you're going to be so strong afterward. So brave. And that's a good thing. You'll be glad to have gone through it. I promise."

"I guess so," I say, tearing up. "I'll try to remember that."

Day three of radiation is our twenty-fifth anniversary. I ceremoniously present Tim with my gift in the morning. He studies the photographs in the cubbies, laughs at the dated hairstyles and the kids in their early years.

"It seems so long ago," he says, his face softening to a smile.

"Another lifetime."

"This is wonderful," he says, looking at me with the sentimental eyes I often long for, but rarely get. Then, after a pause, he stutters, "Uh, I-I thought you said we weren't doing gifts."

His face looks helpless.

"I don't remember saying that." My heart falters.

"Well, I do have a card for you." He walks to the table and hands me an envelope.

The card is a Marc Chagall painting, a bride and groom floating in a dark, indigo sky. I try to study it and appreciate the scene, but since I'm familiar with the painting, it's difficult to focus my attention on it rather than my collapsing interior. Tim has written a few lines inside the card, but they hold no power to lift me. Words are not his thing.

"Thank you for this nice card." I push my voice above the lump that has lodged itself in my throat. I don't want to hurt him, so I give him a hug, avoiding eye contact, and then excuse myself upstairs, tears leaking as soon as I'm out of his sight. I escape to our closet, close the door, and weep silently, not wanting to make a scene.

I'm used to this part of Tim. I know how he hates the Hallmark versions of holidays and celebrations. To him there is no difference between September sixth and September seventh, no specialness to twenty-five years of marriage over twenty-four. Part of me understands and agrees. I can get just as cynical as he is at how our culture has commercialized everything. But I want and need attention and validation. "I love you every day," he would say if pressed to explain. But he doesn't say "I love you" every day because that, too, would come to be expected. He is averse to forced acquiescence—quietly rebellious, as my mother used to call him.

WELL FUCK YOU AND FUCK YOUR CARD. It's not enough. Today it's not enough.

In the afternoon, Tim brings me an exquisite bouquet of dahlias, all shades of pink, each a different variety, but I can't give him credit knowing that Emily picked them out. Tim's parents have given us a gift certificate to a trendy restaurant that the kids have chosen, and on the way there I try to feel excited. When we're seated, it's so dark I struggle to read the menu. We order, but the food takes too long to arrive, and mine doesn't live up to the wait.

At home I am ready to break.

"Today was really hard," I tell Tim once we're alone. "I'll be glad to have it behind me. I just wish you were more sentimental about things like anniversaries."

"But you told me not to get anything. You said I'd done enough for you and that we shouldn't spend the money."

"I must have, but I don't remember it. I'm feeling overwhelmed right now so everything hurts and I'm only at the beginning and I'm already having a hard time and everyone says it gets harder and I don't want to picture that, and I haven't even lined up drivers yet. I've had offers but I can't get it together to make arrangements. And do you think I should offer to pay for gas? Because I figured out that it would come to over $300. More money we don't really have."

"Don't worry," Tim says. "People won't want to be reimbursed. And I could do your schedule but I'm on a deadline with work. Why don't you ask Cole?"

"I guess so," I say, feeling pained that he doesn't swoop in to help. Tim leaves and I wallow in self-pity, replaying the last few days in my head, re-living each hurt.

Enough! You've got to keep moving forward. Go talk to Cole and ask him for help.

I knock on his door. "I'm struggling with something, Cole, and I need your help. Can you set up an online schedule for people to sign up to drive me to radiation?"

"Can't Dad do it?"

"Dad is busy. I know you can do it." I suggest he call my friend who set up the meal schedule last month. "She can walk you through it."

"Why can't she walk *you* through it?"

"I'm asking *you*, Cole. My brain isn't working too well now. I'm overwhelmed, and I need you to do this." My voice falters and the tears roll down.

"Okay Mom, I'll try."

It takes over an hour and two calls to my friend, but he figures it out and I send the e-mail to a group of my contacts to ask for help just before collapsing to bed.

> *Hello Dear Friends,*
>
> *The last few weeks of August saw me getting stronger by the day. There is nothing sweeter than getting your health back! Last week I was declared ready for radiation, which started the day after Labor Day.*
>
> *Looking at the somewhat daunting schedule of thirty-one remaining appointments, I am ready to take people up on their offers to drive me to radiation. Cole created this schedule, which lists all the days I have radiation. Of course, not every day needs to be filled, as Tim, Cole, Emily, and I can take turns as well. This is just for those who can and WANT to participate in this way.*
>
> *I'm sending this to everyone on my update list, and I realize that folks out of town will only be "drivers in spirit." And honestly, I need you, too, to drive alongside ;-).*
>
> *This is humbling and I am so very grateful...*

The next morning I go online to check the schedule. To my amazement, it's almost full. I read down the list, seeing names from all eras and corners of my life. It's as if they are all holding me up—away from the muddy angst of the previous days—and I'm overwhelmed again, this time with awe, buoyed with the first sense of lightness I've felt in days.

Still tender near Tim, though, I hold my distance from him. He approaches just before I leave and hands me a card, a mountain landscape by Georgia O'Keeffe with an orange mound of hills accentuated by curved ridges that brighten the foreground. There is a quotation inside by the artist that reads:

I've been absolutely terrified every moment of my life—and I've never let it keep me from doing a single thing I wanted to do.

"I've never imagined Georgia O'Keeffe that way," I say. "And she's right, you know. You've got to keep going…right through your fear." I give Tim a watery smile. "This is really nice, thank you. Are you going to give me one of these every day?" He shrugs and smiles in reply.

I think about the woman in the Rousseau painting and wonder if she is scared, too. *Maybe we're all afraid, but some of us are better at moving forward anyway. I'm not one of those people. I need help…I've got to ask for help.*

Bear Medicine

September 8 to 12, 2012 • Radiation day 5 to day 7

It's only the first week of radiation and I'm already floundering. Former patients call this a marathon, but I'm not a runner. Physical endurance is not my forte. Even worse, they all say it's easiest in the beginning; the hard part, they say, is the last two weeks, and this worries me because I haven't exactly breezed through the start of this race.

I'm relying on my ability to stay with things—even the hard things—to keep replacing the air down deep in my gut. But I'm struggling. It's not like labor, which stuffs all the pain into one long session and then rewards you with a baby at the end. There is no reward here as far as I can tell, other than surviving it.

My brothers were right. I'm a wimp. It's only fifteen minutes a day; just buck up, sister. You could have it so much worse.

But I know I could have it better, too.

It's the radiation nurse—Ms. Fussy—she's the problem! She's inhuman, uncaring, rule-bound. Why would someone like her be in charge? Where is her compassion, her tenderness? Why won't she try to soften this experience for me somehow?

My younger brother, Paul, calls on Monday. "I'm coming on Wednesday to take you to radiation," he announces.

"But it's your fiftieth birthday. Shouldn't you be with your family? You don't have to do this. I've got a driver already lined up."

"This is what I want to do. I want to take you to radiation," he repeats. I gently chide him, trying to let him off the hook. It seems unnecessary and impractical for him to drive five hours north just to do this for me.

"Tell your hubby he's playing golf with me in the afternoon. And tell Emily to prepare a cake that will make her dad jealous." I see that he has a plan, that he will get something, too. I accept his offer. *We will help him celebrate.*

Wednesday arrives—Paul's birthday and day seven of my thirty-three-day marathon. It's a clear, mild September morning, the kind of day that usually has me humming, but not today. I have barely clicked in the seatbelt of his Volvo sedan before I start in.

"I can't believe this woman. She's so tight-assed, like she's the queen of the place. Yes, I know she's in charge, but you'd think they'd train them to be kind. I mean, *hello there*, we have cancer and it's not like we're going to the spa. It makes me so mad—and I don't want to be mad—but I can't help it. I can't stop thinking that she's got it all wrong. But I don't know how to change it. I'm so bad at complaining you know—it's just not my style. And I swear I feel like I'm being tortured—the whole scene is almost unbelievable. I mean they actually have a metal table with two-inch holes in it that you lie on and apparently no one ever thought, *gee, that might hurt—like, maybe we should soften the edges somehow.* Because let me tell you, every time I'm on that damn thing my shoulder blade lodges into one of the holes and it cuts right into my skin because they only put a sheet over it—and it might as well be nothing. I swear I have red marks on my back for an hour afterward—and I've mentioned this to two different doctors, and they both just laughed and said, 'Oh, you just need to gain some weight.' And I felt like slapping them. Can you believe it? They're clueless! And I don't know, bro, I just don't know what to do."

We are heading southeast, into the morning sun. Paul sighs, reaches for his aviators, and flips down the visor of the car.

"You just have to break its back," he says.

"Umm, I'm not sure what you mean by that."

"You count off each day to the halfway point, and when you get there you'll have broken its back. You'll be on the other side, and then things will get easier."

"That might work for you, but remember, I'm a wimp. You've always thought so and you were right. Anyway, I'm sorry I'm dumping all this on you."

"Hey sis, that's why I'm here. And you're wrong. You're stronger than you think." His dark blue eyes hold a knowing but weary twinkle. His expression and his body do not hide the trials he's been carrying for the last fifteen years, layers that have taken an emotional toll and added more than fifty pounds to his muscular physique, all since the day that changed everything, the day his infant daughter Katelyn had her first grand mal seizure and was airlifted to Children's Hospital in Boston.

"So how is Katie? Has anything improved—you know—since her new med routine?"

"Well, Mo…" He sighs, and his face winces a little, as it usually does when he speaks of her. "Katelyn is Katelyn." He doesn't like to talk about it, and whenever I ask him, these vague, brief replies are standard. I can see that it hurts him to talk about her, but I feel uncaring if I don't ask.

"Well, I hope something good comes of it. I hope she'll have a positive response." He shrugs his shoulders as I let him know that our exit is next.

"Well, here we go. It's time to knock another day off my count. Turn right at that sign."

"Hey, is there a grocery store nearby?" Paul asks as he parks the car and turns off the engine.

I give him directions, assuming he's off to get a doughnut or some other confection. I stifle the urge to nag and instead turn my attention to the bright, blue September light blazing on the shrubs and trees surrounding the parking lot.

Paul gets out of the Volvo and lumbers toward the back of the car where he meets me, arms outstretched. He enfolds me in one of his famous bear hugs—tender, sustained, protective. He rocks me and murmurs endearingly. Then he retracts his arms, bending his elbows backward at shoulder level, and forming his hands into fists. He tilts his forehead to make contact with mine and waits for me to mirror his stance. As the sister of this former football player, I remember how to do this. Soon I hear a deep, throaty GRRRRR rumbling from the base of brother bear's throat. "GRRRR...GRRRR...GRRRR," he growls. I start to feel a little awkward, aware that someone might see us and think we're strange. But he keeps on, pulling me toward the vibration of his call, taking me into his bristly fur, his musky warmth, his sinewy brawn. He is grizzly, mighty, conquering, and his GRRRR is pouring in, filling my tiny shell, entering cell and muscle, blood and bone.

He starts again and this time I join him. "GRRRR...GRRRRRR...GRRRRRRRR..." The tremors begin beneath us, then move upward and outward—trembling through my limbs, surging up my spine.

GRRRRRRRR...I am wild...rugged...fearless...

GRRRRRRRRRRR...I am mountainous...limitless...free...

As I enter the building, I'm part bear—right? So I'm protected—I mean, how many wimpy bears do you know? And I'm not talking about cartoon bears or teddy bears. I'm talking about grizzlies—the baddest bears out there—yeah, that's me. And when I see Ms. Fussy I give her the look—you know—the "don't mess with me" look, and when the table cuts into me, I'm like, *are you kidding? That's nothing, just a flicker. And I've got fish to catch, people, so I'm outta here.*

"That was a good session, bro," I tell Paul when I rejoin him in the parking lot. "You really helped. I'm so glad you're here."

I open the passenger door of his Volvo to find an enormous purple aster sitting on my seat. "It's stunning. I love it! And look at you, giving *me* a present, and it's *your* birthday. Well, lunch is on me, bro—lobster rolls at Reds, right?"

We've been waiting in line for forty-five minutes at this iconic, coastal Maine fish shack. When we reach the front canopy, and become third in line, a voice comes over the loudspeaker. "Thank you all for waiting in line today. How 'bout if the next person from Massachusetts gets a free lunch."

I can't believe our luck. I'm so tickled that I insist on telling the woman that it's Paul's fiftieth, and she's all over it. "Well, folks," she announces, "looks like we've got our winner, and he's a birthday boy, too. Ayup, fifty years old today. How about if we sing him our best Happy Birthday?"

It's high noon when the chorus of strangers serenades Paul. He's bathed in glorious sunshine, grinning and nodding and waving to the crowd, who smile and cheer as if we're one big family, and in that moment, we are.

The Healing Table

September 13, 2012 • Radiation day 8

There's a massage table in our bedroom, on loan from a friend for as long as I need it. The table is nearly new, with birch legs and a well-padded top. Linda, a long-time friend, used the table first, just after my surgery in July, to administer Jin Shin Jyutsu for three consecutive days. Her treatments focused on releasing any lingering anesthesia or other medications from my body tissues, and part way through each session I felt a sense of movement return, as if leaves and twigs were being lifted from a stream so the water could flow again.

Today, a man named Rowan has come to give me a massage. The coordinator at our local high school's Wellness Room, where I volunteer, Rowan is training to become a massage therapist. This means he needs guinea pigs, and he has asked me to be one of them, offering a massage every other week during my radiation period.

When Rowan arrives, I know he's on a tight schedule, so I don't waste time asking him the story behind his tattooed arms, colors faded like a print in the sun. We both have cause to feel a little awkward: He's early on in his training, and I'm a one-breasted, recovering Catholic whose skin he is about to touch.

Rowan leaves the room while I undress and slide under the thin cotton blanket. I've never received a therapeutic massage from a man before, so I'm actively replacing all the guilty associations with pure ones. *There is nothing wrong. Rowan is here to learn and practice. I deserve this.*

When Rowan returns, he asks if I would like an eye bag and music.

"Yes, thank you."

He rifles through his tote bag and pulls out a blue eye bag and a base for his smart phone. Moments later, notes of ethereal music join the flow of warm air coming through the open windows, and I'm breathing in the scent of lavender from the eye bag.

Rowan has been a cabinetmaker, an artisan bread baker, and most recently a Reiki master. He begins the session by cradling the crown of my head with his hands. Within moments, the comforting heat I associate with Reiki is entering my body and I deepen my breathing in response. He keeps his hands in this position for a few minutes and then moves to the other end of the table, where he lifts the covers off my right leg and tucks them under my left.

With eyes closed, my awareness of sound, smell, and touch are heightened. I hear the flick of the pourer spout lift and the glug-glug of the massage oil pour into his hands, which rub together a few times and then touch down on my right foot. His warm fingers glide across my skin, anointing my arch, ankles, and toes with oil.

One more click-glug-glug marks the next area of focus, where he presses into the tendons and muscles of each leg, from denseness of calf to softness of inner thigh. My body sways in response, a motion that frees me from the rigid stillness I must endure in the radiation position.

He attends to my arms, hands, and shoulders, removes the eye bag, then asks me to roll over. I open my eyes to see the bands of sunlight on the pine floors. He pulls back the covers, baring my skin to the reassuring attention of his hands, which work the concave and convex surfaces of my back, intuitively finding their way to the knots, caring for each of them until they—and much of the tension that has accumulated from the last two weeks—are gone. With his touch, he is replacing the contracted, dark associations of the radiation table with softness, ease, and warmth.

"You can turn back over now," he says gently. Once I do, his fingertips land lightly on my face, then press along my cheekbones and facial muscles, gradually moving to the outer edges, around my ears and lastly, to my scalp, which tingles in response to the spiraling motion. He replaces the eye bag and works the front of my shoulders and neck.

His hands come to rest where they began, on the crown of my head. He stays there long enough to allow the flow of warmth to course through my body again, to make sure that every cell has been touched. At last, he lifts his hands almost imperceptibly and says, "Take your time, Maureen. I'll wait outside."

With this gift of massage, Rowan has offered me a respite from the trials of being a cancer patient. His tenderness has stroked my heart and body, filling my senses with pleasure. He has erased the pain and indignity of the radiation chamber, at least for now.

"Thank you, Rowan. This is just what I needed."

THE LIGHT FROM HERE

Counting the Days

September 13 to 26, 2012 • Radiation day 9 to day 18

My brother told me to count the days, that my marathon would get easier after I broke its back. And now I'm at day nine, with eight more to go to the halfway point.

Counting becomes the structure of my day—my rhythm. Rise at 6:30; meditate for twenty minutes; eat, wash, and receive my daily card from Tim; wait for the driver (who arrives at 8:50); travel for fifty-eight minutes; pee, change, and wait; get called in at 10 a.m. Most days, the hood whirrs for about fifteen minutes. Some days they do an extra treatment called a boost to intensify the rays. Either way, I'm home by noon and I cross another day off, drawing a bold "x" through the box on my calendar.

The hardest part is the time on the table, when the nerve pain in my shoulder screams at me to adjust my position to lessen the pain, and I can't.

"Have you tried listening to music?" my friend Lorraine asks. "That might help distract you."

"They've got the radio going, but it doesn't make a difference."

"No, that won't do. You need an iPod with the music *you* choose in your ears, nice and loud, too."

"I don't have an iPod."

"I'll lend you mine." She drops it off the next day.

I choose a few peaceful, melodic songs for my playlist, thinking they will relax me, but on the table the next day I feel as raw as ever.

"I think I need a more dancy playlist," I tell Tim that evening. "Will you help me?"

As he plays tunes from his laptop, I listen and choose songs that make me want to get up and groove. The next day—eyes closed, earbuds in, lying on the hard, sharp metal—I'm transported, smiling as the refrain of one of my songs reminds me over and again, "You might as well be walkin' on the sun."

There are six songs on my *Radiant* playlist, all of them catchy and spirited. One of my favorites is an oldie called *Rawhide*, sung by Frankie Laine. I love how his deep voice rides over the steady background beat like a cowboy driving the herd. His singing takes me from the radiation chamber to the open blaze of the West.

> *Keep movin', movin', movin',*
> *Though they're disapprovin',*
> *Keep them doggies movin' Rawhide!*
> *Don't try to understand 'em,*

Just rope and throw and grab 'em,

Soon we'll be living high and wide.

My heart's calculatin'

My true love will be waitin', be waiting at the end of my ride.

On day seventeen I pass the halfway point. The next morning I rise lighter, sensing that the slope of my journey has changed and I'm shifting downhill, ever so slightly. Tim presents me with a card just before my driver (Kalla today) arrives to pick me up. The painting on the card is by Miró, one of the surrealists, and I know Kalla will love it.

Kalla is Finnish, with mid-length, Scandinavian-blonde hair that she pulls up in twin buns on top of her head. She is an artist and designer, and her style is like Miró's, breaking rules of scale, color, and content. *The work must be conceived with fire in the soul* are the words inside, a quotation by Miró that Tim has chosen. *Kalla should see this.* I grab all eighteen of my cards and bring them to show her.

Once we are underway, Kalla asks me how I am doing.

"Did you know that my radiation treatments started on the week of our twenty-fifth wedding anniversary?"

"Oh, that sounds like fun," Kalla groans.

"I was kind of a wreck that week. I was just getting my bounce back after surgery and then I had to re-enter treatment—and I didn't want to at all—and then the anniversary came.

"And Tim doesn't get into giving presents on birthdays and anniversaries. He thinks it's too forced. I know how much he hates the pressure, so supposedly I told him months before our anniversary that he was off the hook. He was so good to me all summer and at the time, I guess I thought he had done enough."

"But I didn't remember saying this, Kalla, not at all, so when the big day came and he only gave me a card, I just crumbled." Kalla's eyes flash me a glance of knowing sympathy. "But I got through. It was a relief to put it behind me. And then, a wonderful thing happened. He started giving me these cards." I glance down at the pile in my lap.

"Each morning he presents me with a new one. He designs and prints them himself. And now I have eighteen—one for each day of radiation. I brought them for you to look at while I'm inside."

"There are bare-breasted women," I explain as I thumb through the cards, "a lot of redheads and red-orange color themes, and soothing landscapes—they're all so 'me'—and there's a quotation by each artist inside the card, and Tim chooses those just for me, too."

Kalla laughs and nods approvingly.

"It's one of the best presents he's ever given me." I want Kalla to understand why, so I recount the details of our fight about Tim not posting the notice of my art show on Facebook. "I think the cards are Tim's way of telling me he believes in me as an artist. I know I shouldn't need this affirmation, but I do."

"Of course you do, darling. You're only human."

I wipe my eyes. I've been tearing up a lot lately.

"Thanks for listening, Kalla—and for being my driver today. I was so happy when you signed up."

"Are you kidding?" she says. "There's no place I'd rather be."

When I get home I tell Tim about my morning. I show him the calendar with eighteen days crossed off, then I grin and GRRRR and he joins me.

Move 'em on, head 'em up

Head 'em up, move 'em on

Move 'em on, head 'em up

Rawhide

Count 'em out, ride 'em in,

Ride 'em in, count 'em out,

Count 'em out, ride 'em in

Rawhide!

Soul Friends

September 27 to October 5 • Radiation day 19 to day 24

I'm past the halfway mark, but the weeks ahead loom. Each morning I stand, raise my hands in fists, and rumble a series of GRRRRs. This never fails, partly because it makes me feel strong (a handy trick, like putting your arms in a power position), and partly because it makes me laugh. *Look at me. I'm such a toughie.*

Someone new drives me almost every day. Most are women, each from a different stage of my life—pre-marriage, mothering, work. Some are good friends, but others are acquaintances I've wanted to know better. Either way, our two hours in the car allow us to take a step closer to each other. The circumstances lend themselves to an intimacy and truthfulness that I prefer over small talk.

My friend Becky drives me on one of my weekly check-up days, a post-treatment consult with one of the oncologists at the center. I pictured I would be meeting with my radiation oncologist each week, a smart, sensitive woman who is the main reason I chose this center, but it turns out that all the doctors take turns. Today is my third check-up and the third different male doctor who minimizes my difficulties, cajoling me to gain weight to pad the table.

When I return to the car I'm close to tears. Becky is waiting for me and when she hears my plight, she frowns, lifting her brow so understandingly that I fall into weeping. She strokes my back and waits while I sob.

Joanna, a nurse and former neighbor who has known me since before I was married, has signed up for three drives. She asks questions I don't even know I have, checks my incision, and consults with an oncology colleague after seeing me to ascertain whether I'm progressing normally.

She is as bronze as I am fair and asks to check my skin. She nods when I say, "I can't get used to the notion that this scorching will help me. Fifty-one years of 'no burn' brainwashing can't be undone in a couple of weeks."

"What are you using on your skin?"

"I'm putting stuff on all day." I describe my whole routine, starting with the aloe I apply in the changing room just after I pop a peppermint Tums (both offer a sense of cooling). I repeat the aloe whenever the stinging gets distracting, which is every few hours. At bedtime, I coat myself with Aquaphor, a gooey petroleum ointment that adheres to my T-shirt, turning it cold and stain-soaked by morning.

"I hate the stuff, but everyone says it works the best."

"You're doing it right. Just keep at it," Joanna says. "And be careful to stay out of the sun. You still have weeks to go."

Betsy is my backup driver, taking me twice on short notice. She has a lilting Virginia drawl, a grizzly-sized SUV, and a close friend from home who has just been diagnosed with breast cancer.

"She's not like you," she explains. "She doesn't seem to want to talk about it or reach out for help."

"I understand. At first I felt uncomfortable accepting assistance—too much guilt—but now I'm quite used to it. People will do almost anything to help someone with cancer, and I've learned to just let that in. To be honest, it will be hard to have that part end."

But soon it will end, and I want to start preparing for what comes next. By coincidence, my five months of active cancer treatment will conclude in late October, just as my time to paint begins.

I start preparing by straightening my workspace: arranging books, filing art clippings, and sorting through the prints of all my paintings. In the process, I find the invitation from last year's show, featuring a painting called *Soul Friends*. I study the image. I realize that in a way, it tells my story, showing what I went through before my diagnosis and what I am going through now.

I made the painting to help me deal with my anxiety. I started with mountains (always a comfort), then added three big symbols: the tree of life with its spiraling branches to remind me of the connection of earth to the divine; a colorful temple to help me approach the future I feared; and a great white bear, who would guard and keep me safe. The bear I conjured was an amalgam of the fierce, warrior polar bear from *The Golden Compass* (which I read with the children when they were young) and a spirit bear, which is an albino black bear protected by the native peoples on islands along the Pacific Northwest coast. In the studio, these symbols helped me believe I had the grit to make it through my anxious place and toward a future in which I had the courage to offer my heart freely and fully.

In the early stages of creating the painting, I showed myself riding on the bear's back, where I felt most secure. But in the final week of working on it, I realized that I needed to dismount and take the last steps on my own, so I painted myself off the bear. In the final version I am stepping across the threshold of the temple, reaching my arm back to acknowledge what carried me, and what I will keep in my heart as I move forward.

I realize now that creating this painting—and others like it last year—helped me to prepare for my cancer journey. It trained me to redirect my nervous energy, to move through the wall of fear using creative thought and intentional action. The bear painting offers another parallel to my situation. Like the bear, my friends take me to the building and wait, but they cannot go in and lie on the table for me. That task is solely mine and doing it is part of my medicine.

Lately, as I lie on the radiation table, I understand that nothing has changed other than me. The metal is still sharp, the room still cold, and my shoulder still aches unmercifully. But now I know that these things are not separate from me and are not anyone's fault. They just *are*, and I am strangely grateful to them because they have forced me to pull from a deeper source. During my long slog through anxiety the two years before my cancer came, I honed my ability to breathe, wait, and trust that something would come, an image, idea, or person that would guide me forward—like the bear did.

While I wait, I try to notice and feel what I'm grateful for. The way the hummingbird zips through the garden and stops at anything purple; the effortless conversation about art that I just had with my friend/driver Holly; the e-mail a friend sent me last week offering free acupuncture to support my body through radiation. The signs are everywhere when I remember to look for them.

Constellation of Kindness

October 6 to 16, 2012 • Radiation day 25 to day 30

It's the Saturday before my last week of radiation, and I'm running errands in Camden village when I notice my friend Mary rushing toward me.

"I can't believe it's you," she says. She hands me a shopping bag, looks around to make sure no one is watching, then leans in. "I just bought this for you. It's a padded bra. Don't feel you have to wear it, but I thought, well, maybe you might like one."

I put it on as soon as I get home and parade around the house like Beyoncé, acting so saucy that Tim points out, "You should have gotten one of those years ago."

"I always wanted to wear one, but never dared," I confess. "I don't care what people think now. It's silly I ever did."

"The strangest thing is happening," I tell an acquaintance over breakfast in a cafe overlooking Camden Harbor. "I'm the Benjamin Button of radiation—going backward like he did, getting stronger rather than weaker as I progress."

Like others, Jana has stepped in to do something nice, treating me to a meal and a listening ear. I explain to her how well I feel, even though I'm nearing the fifth week of treatment, the point when most are starting to flag. She asks me why.

"Good food, rest, and acupuncture all help, but there's something bigger going on. I'm happier than I have felt in years, and I think it's because of all the kindness.

"Early on I realized that this is my chance to receive—without guilt or the pressure to reciprocate. People *want* and *need* to help, you know.

"I wouldn't want to wish cancer on anyone, of course, but right now I feel grateful for mine. I've never been treated so well or let myself receive like this before, and it has changed me. I feel like I've touched the very core of love."

A belief system can be worn away by small acts that defy it. Like when a friend of a friend, a woman I barely know, offers to massage my feet.

"I heard about your diagnosis," she says to me. "I offer foot reflexology to cancer patients, no charge."

She lives in a trailer with tidy furnishings and homemade art on the walls. She is old enough to be my mother, but moves lithely as she places the basin of hot water at my feet.

"I added some drops of lavender essential oil," she says. "Just get comfortable, dear, and rest your feet in the water. I'll be back in ten minutes for the massage."

This stream of kindness has flowed since the very beginning of my diagnosis, and its current has succeeded in unfurling the grip that has held me all of my life, the belief that I am lacking—money, strength, and most of all, love. Each act, each gesture is like a star in a constellation I've never seen before, but have always wanted to believe in. And now, seeing it stretch so clearly overhead, I can no longer deny its existence.

Looking Ahead

October 17 to 20, 2012 • Radiation day 31 to day 33

"I look like a piece of modern art," I say to Tim, referring to the trapezoid of red across my left chest, bisected by the uneven line of my incision.

"Your scar looks even cooler now," Tim remarks. "How is it feeling today?"

"It's the same—stinging and hot—until it starts to itch. It's driving me crazy, but no bother, it will be better soon. The end felt unreachable six weeks ago, but now it's so close."

"Only four more days 'till you're a free woman," Tim declares.

"I can't wait."

"What happens next?"

"I've got an appointment with the oncologist the week after I'm done. The last phase of treatment is five years of hormonal therapy."

"What's that?"

"It's pills, and I don't want to take them. I'm going to talk to Dr. Barb and see what she says."

On my second-to-last day of radiation, I arise jiggly and weak. I feel like I did when I ran a half mile in gym class for the Presidential Fitness Awards in seventh grade, my body burning and buzzing so crazily by the end that it felt like I wasn't running anymore, just falling forward arrhythmically, strength gone, driven only by will.

I am relieved that Audrey, a long-time friend and former coworker, is driving today. Her soft British accent and gentle green eyes are as comforting as the warm soup she used to serve her preschoolers.

"I was doing so well, Audrey, until this morning when I woke up slobbering head to toe. I think I've run out of gas, so I'm not sure I'll be much company this morning."

"You're just a bit soggy, that's all," she soothes. "Lord knows; I would be if I were you."

"I'm so happy I made it through, it's like I'm flooding. And everyone has been so kind. Like you—all your cards and e-mails—I felt you with me every day."

"Ohhh, there now," Audrey says. "I kept thinking of you, so I would write a quick note to let you know. It was nothing."

"But all those nothings, they piled up. They helped keep me going."

At the center, Dawn greets me with her usual smile, asking me how I'm doing—as she does every day.

"I'm the marathon runner collapsing at the finish line."

"I'm not surprised. I've been amazed at how energetic you've stayed these last few weeks. Tomorrow you're done, though. Good job, Maureen."

"Thank you for cheering me on, Dawn. You really made a difference." Tears are leaking as I tell her. I don't bother to hide them.

"It's been my pleasure. I love my job."

I cry throughout the day. I'm not sad, just unraveling, unable to stop the release. I wonder if I'll be crawling and bawling like this for weeks, but the next morning I wake revived, like Superman post-Kryptonite. Tim does the last drive and hears me say, "It's over, I've made it, I'm done," the whole way there.

I find the final session easy, knowing that every moment of discomfort is nearly the last. I bring a selection of my art prints as a thank-you for the staff, letting each person choose their favorite. Outside, Tim captures me doing one last GRRR for the camera. I can't stop smiling.

A yellow rose, wrapped in tissue paper and tied with ribbon, is resting on our front porch table upon our return.

"It's so beautiful," I say, showing the exquisitely formed flower to Tim. I check the card to see who has delivered it: someone who knows what it's like to finish this marathon as well as I do.

My friend Linda calls that afternoon. She's a yoga teacher and body worker—the one who gave me the idea of replacing the word cancer with "my project" at the very beginning. I still remember how relieved I felt—even excited—when I realized I could turn my diagnosis into something creative.

"I'm ready for your yoga retreat," I tell Linda. "I'm planning to begin phase two of my project: I want to make a book of paintings and stories to share with others who are going through this."

I have attended these retreats before—three days of yoga, nourishing meals, and walks, located on a nearby island. When the flyer announcing this one arrived the previous month, I knew I wanted to be there and wanted to bring Emily too, to thank her for caring for me during the many months of treatment. I wasn't sure she would be interested, but when she saw the flyer on the kitchen counter, she said, "This looks great Mom. Are you going?"

"Yes. Would you like to go too?"

She surprised me by giving a firm "yes." We didn't have the money for this, so I sold my mother's silver to pay for it. Polishing silver has never been my thing, and I didn't need to worry that my mother—lost in a world of dementia now—would question what I was doing.

Now that my active treatment is over, I know I need to prepare for the next phase of my life. The high I'm feeling will not last. The drivers, gift givers, meal makers, and card senders will turn away from me—as is natural—toward someone else in need. It's time to shift my focus back to making art.

Return to Life

November 2012 through April 2013 (six months)

At the island yoga retreat, I spend hours alone in the designated quiet area, the formal dining room in the ten-bedroom home where we stay. I sit at the far end of a massive mahogany table, surrounded on three sides by tall, satin-draped windows overlooking the ocean. I sink into the silence, spreading index cards on the table, waiting for stories from my cancer experience to distill in my mind so I can scribble notes on the cards. The images come—on walks, in downward dog pose, or staring at the sea. I leave the retreat with piles of ideas.

As soon as I get home, I dive in, writing and painting, taking advantage of the month-long breather I have before I must decide about the next leg of treatment—hormonal therapy. During that month, I meet with my oncologist and with Dr. Barb. Both present statistics supporting the benefits of hormonal therapy in reducing the recurrence of breast cancer in women whose malignant cells were dependent on the hormones estrogen and/or progesterone. Hormonal therapy is the final phase of treatment for breast cancer and is usually taken for five years. Both doctors acknowledge the common side effects, but downplay them.

"Just try it," Dr. Barb urges. "If your body doesn't tolerate the medicine, you can stop it or try a different medicine. If it does, you'll have the extra protection."

In my month of waiting, I push the decision from my mind. It unsettles me to dwell on it. During this time, Cole and Emily move out of the house, he to Colorado, she to Vermont. We are all ready to shift into a new phase, so their leaving feels as right for me as it does for them.

I slide into my studio as often as I can—between work stints, before meals, and in the quiet November mornings and evenings. I brush colors on canvas and lay words on paper, moving back and forth from one to the other as freely as the leaves falling from the trees by my studio. There is power in the newness and enthusiasm of my quest, and I step innocently and exuberantly, unencumbered by the critic.

December arrives. Short days, cold winds. It's time to decide.

My medical team has persuaded me to be brave and give the medicine a try, even though my inner alarm sounds whenever I picture it. To counter my aversion, I tell myself this is what I want, that I'm doing it for my kids—and hypothetical grandkids.

I begin taking the meds in early December, just as Tim and I travel to see my mother and my family in Massachusetts. The "memory-care facility" where my mother lives is having a holiday party and several of my siblings will attend. When Tim and I exit the elevator at the third floor, I barely recognize the unit—usually quiet—now full of holiday decorations, music, and chattering visitors.

It takes a minute to locate Mom, who is in her wheelchair, head slumped forward despite the party that pulses around her. I lean down and kiss her on the cheek to wake her. Her eyes open and when she sees me she starts laughing, her face full of joy. It's always like this when she sees me now; her love is unencumbered, free from past hurts.

Two of my brothers, a sister-in-law, and a nephew arrive. We choose a round table near the kitchen and sit down to wait for the meal. I take a spot next to Mom and wrap my hands around hers, our eyes locked in connection. In the past, my mother was never the one I turned to for support—her stoicism offered little comfort. Dementia has made her softer, lighter, and more openly loving. Sitting so near, I feel the need to have my mother know what I'm going through. I doubt she'll understand, but I want to try.

"I've had a mastectomy, Mom," I say, my mouth close to her ear. My words are overlaid by those from the singer across the room, and Mom looks puzzled.

I try again. "I've had breast cancer, Mom. Just like you."

She looks at me, showing a deep and complex tenderness. Her eyes flicker with understanding and she says, deliberately, "So you…got it…from me."

I lean into her, pressing my one-breasted chest against her one-breasted chest, a well of love rising to fill us both.

Back home in Maine, in the flurry of the holidays, between work and studio time, I watch for side effects from the medicine. I notice a few common ones—hot flashes and vaginal discharge—but they are bearable. As Christmas, New Year's, and snowstorms pass, though, I don't notice the ever-so-slight emotional descent that occurs each day. Instead, I ruminate about the stressors in my life:

Christmas is always hard.

Mom is running out of money. I can't bear the thought of moving her to a nursing home.

I've had so much attention during my treatment. It's hard to have it end.

This painting is awful. I don't like it at all.

Why isn't anyone calling me?

It isn't until mid-January that I connect the dots. I am standing by the window in my bedroom, staring out at the backyard, glazed in white. It's a Saturday afternoon and I feel as barren as the garden below.

Who is this person by the window? I don't recognize her, have never before experienced the complete hollowness she feels. *This isn't me.* I recall how many times I have cried this week, how I have stopped painting, how I have not called anyone to talk about my sunken heart or to go for a walk. *Who would want to be around me now? I am too much of a downer.*

A moment of clear thinking comes and I wonder if the hormonal therapy is the cause of my desolation. *I will call my oncologist on Monday and ask for permission to stop. I want to prevent cancer recurrence but not if I'm going to feel like this.*

At dinner that night I skip the pill. I do the same the next day. Monday comes and I do not call the oncologist. *She will want me to try another type of the same medication, and I'm too weak to plead my case.* Instead, I call the acupuncturist I saw during radiation. I tell her about the response I've had to the hormonal therapy. "It's been five weeks and I'm depressed in a strange way, like I've been drugged. I want to help my body flush the meds out of my system."

As gradually as they gripped me, the crying, the desolation, the feelings of unworthiness dissipate, until by March I am well again. When I'm feeling strong enough, I see Dr. Barb. I tell her I've stopped taking the hormonal therapy. Together, we experiment with alternatives until we find a protocol of supplements, dietary changes, and exercise that have been shown in some studies to reduce the risk of recurrence, with tolerable side effects. Later, when I see my oncologist, she accepts my choice without laying on any guilt—she knows and trusts Dr. Barb.

Through it all, I paint and write, expanding the phrases I wrote at the retreat into chapters for my book project, choosing several of them to further explore on canvas. The process and the connection to images and words are like a flow of water washing me clean.

Sharing My Story
May 2013

By May, I have finished the first phase of my project, a group of paintings and chapters that tell some of my cancer stories. There are more to come, but not until next winter.

Tim offers to make a booklet to showcase the new work. "We can offer it at the opening," he says, smiling. "People are going to want them." My heart swells recalling the journey we've made together this year, how it has taken us to this moment of celebration.

A friend helps me hang my show at a coffee shop in Camden. Surveying my paintings lined up on the sunlit walls, I feel like a mother parading her children in their best clothes, faces washed, shoes shined. It's a cheerful scene, and I'm proud.

On the afternoon of the opening reception a couple of days later, Cole, who is back home for the summer, helps me transform the coffee shop into a real gallery. We move the tables and chairs into a storage room, reserving a few for the platters of hors d'oeuvres and drinks we've brought.

An hour later, the space is filled with chatter and laughter. The door opens steadily and many guests stream in, including Emily and a posse of her friends.

The crowd grows, and I brighten with the energy they bring. I've planned to give a short talk like the one I gave last year. When it's time, I bring down the din and gather my visitors' attention.

"Thank you all for coming. It moves me to see everyone here." As I scan the room, I put my hands on my heart. My throat catches when I see the faces and feel their warmth. Surges of gratitude and joy fill me completely.

Held in this love, I begin.

END

THE LIGHT FROM HERE

Parting Shot
August 2013

The indigo water was calling me, even from 15 feet below. Tim and I were standing with friends on the Bayside Pier in Northport, which at low tide towered over the glassy inner harbor, calm in the late afternoon light.

"Who wants to go swimming?" I called out, aware that to do so meant changing into my bathing suit in public.

"Tim, will you hold up my towel so I can stand in the corner here and have a bit of privacy?"

The late August sun still held plenty of heat, and the weathered decking felt warm underfoot as I walked cautiously along the edge of the pier, feeling the pull to leap off. It scared, but thrilled me to imagine being so daring.

"I want to jump, Tim, but I need you to hold my hand 'til I let go, okay?"

Gripping firmly, I stepped over the upper ledge to a board two feet closer to the water. The moments before the plunge made me remember something Elinor had said to me when I was reluctant to start my radiation treatment a year earlier.

"You'll be amazed at how strong you are when this is all over."

"Weeeee!" I squealed, letting go of Tim's hand as I pushed off, plugged my nose, and penciled through the air. I knew as soon as I hit the salty water that I had to jump again. This time I stood solo on the highest point and reveled in the drop even more. After the third jump, my kid-like glee had convinced Tim that he couldn't miss out on all the fun.

All through my post-cancer summer I rose early to stroll through my garden, noticing the silkiness of peonies, the purple/blue of the baptisia, the sweet wafts of the alyssum. Even the brown piles of worm casings in the raised beds, perfect beads of nourishment, made my heart glad. I felt the power of my limbs and the strength of my lungs as I hiked up Bald Mountain, walked around Beauchamp Point, swam in Lake Megunticook. I poured warmth over my clients, friends, and family, hugging tightly, delighting more freely, dropping the need to be anything other than present, for the simple joy to be *here*.

In Gratitude

This book was four years in the making. At each step there were guides and friends, and I'm sure I couldn't have done this without them.

Kathrin Seitz, my writing teacher and coach, pushed me to stay with the project, to go deeper, to "make art!" She is my favorite cheerleader.

My writing group—Laura Bonazzoli, Franziska Hart, Betsy Perry, Judi Valentine, and Sandy Weisman—traveled with me for three years, offering thoughtful edits, helpful insights, and true kindness. They are in large part responsible for me getting to this place. Thanks doesn't quite cover the breadth of my gratitude.

Sheila Polson was the project's bookends, giving early editorial feedback and final polishing to the manuscript. In addition, Laura Bonazzoli edited for content and style with precision, artistry, and care.

Clare Morin adroitly ushered the second edition of the book to wider audiences. Her belief in the book rivaled—and some days, surpassed—my own. I will always be grateful.

My medical team were all professionals with heart. I honor Dr. Barbara MacDonald, Brien Davis, Dr. Nancy Webb, Dr. Melinda Molin, Cathy McDonald,

Elizabeth Huebener, Dr. Celine Godin, and Dr. Elizabeth Connelly for their intelligent, thorough, and respectful caregiving.

I received several complementary therapies—from Reiki to acupuncture—that offered support and a respite during my treatment period. Sincere appreciation goes to Linda Shepard, Gloria Flynn, Rowan Blaisdell, Nancy Nutt, Monica Shields, and Maggie Churchill for their sensitivity and generosity.

I offer heartfelt thanks to all the meal makers, radiation drivers, and bearers of kindness for lightening my load. Friends, neighbors, and family were all GRRREAT!

The ladies I assist, ages 73 to 96, are like family to me. I thank Elinor, Marny, Marge, Marya, and Gayle for bringing out the best in my heart. They help me laugh and love in the simplest and most beautiful ways. Their belief in me is the ground I walk on.

My friends Elphie, Maggie, Esperanza, Becky, Gloria, Linda, Judy, Mary, Kris, Liz, Susan, Janet, Lorraine, Michael, Kam and Nan give generously, challenge judiciously, and nourish my soul unfailingly. They all have a piece of my heart. Thanks!

My brothers and my in-laws are long-distance love bearers. I treasure them all, especially Timothy Paul Egan (Paul, in the book) for bringing me the GRRRR, and George Ann Seymour, who never let up the caring.

I thank Sue Nugent for cherishing the stories I create on canvas.

Cole's and Emily's presence in my life blesses me with warmth, playfulness, and humor. They show me what love means, and I am deeply grateful to be their mamma.

Tim honors all of my work—as an artist, mother, elder helper, writer, gardener—and NEVER pressures me to make money from my art. I thank him for giving me that space, and for being my patient, steady partner. He was here all the way to the completed book, which he—with his own hands—designed. I'm grateful with all my heart.

Lastly, I thank the teachers who offer instruction on how to breathe through suffering, transform pain into understanding, or just show up in our vulnerable little bodies and love however we are able. Their words lift, push, and inspire me to step more fully into my being.

List of plates

page 2—Love Breaking Through

page 6—Sensing the Way

page 14—Held by the Pines

page 20—Resonance

page 26—The Seed Within

page 34—Guardian of the Lotus Girl

page 42—Lifted

page 46—Transcendence

page 52—The Light From Here

page 58—The Sisters Tree

page 62—Nourishment

page 70—Letting Go in the Grove

page 76—Sanctuary

page 82—As Above, So Below

page 92—Rest

page 100—Nurturance

page 108—What the Heart Knows

page 118—Waiting with the Monarchs

page 126—Intuition

page 134—Brave Little One

page 144—Bear Medicine

page 152—Healing

page 158—Individuality

page 164—Soul Friends

page 170—Constellation of Kindness

page 174—Devotion

page 180—Encircling Moon

page 186—The Way Forward

Prints of all images available at Eganart.com

About the Author

Maureen Egan is an artist, author, and elder caregiver whose creative projects fuse writing and storytelling with imagery. As a painter, Egan uses color and symbolism to express mood and offer a vision. As a writer and storyteller, she charts the human experience in all of its vivid honesty. Egan lives with her husband in Rockport, Maine, near their two grown children.

Born in Massachusetts and a graduate of Holy Cross, Egan worked as an illustrator for the first part of her career. She then became Enrollment Director of the Ashwood Waldorf School in Rockport, Maine, a role she held for more than a decade. In the late 2000s, Egan returned to her roots as an artist, balancing the introspective artistic path by serving as a companion to several elderly women. Her paintings have been shown in galleries throughout the Camden area and her writing has been published in *PenBay Pilot*, *The Camden Herald*, and the quarterly journal *Wellspring*—an educational publication which Egan founded and edited in the 2000s.

www.ingramcontent.com/pod-product-compliance
Lightning Source LLC
Chambersburg PA
CBHW061142010526
44118CB00026B/2843